GEOGRAPHY THE PRIMARY SCHOOL

JOHN BALE

The Author

John Bale is Lecturer in Education at the University of Keele. He has taught at schools in London and Hertfordshire and at Avery Hill College, London. His previous books for school pupils include *The Location of Manufacturing Industry* (Oliver & Boyd, 1981), *Patterns of Underdevelopment* (Nelson, 1982) and *Office Location* (Nelson, 1983).

Subjects in the Primary School
Series editor: Professor John Eggleston

English in the Primary School Tricia Evans
Geography in the Primary School John Bale

GEOGRAPHY IN THE PRIMARY SCHOOL

JOHN BALE

Routledge & Kegan Paul
London

First published in 1987 by
Routledge & Kegan Paul Ltd
11 New Fetter Lane, London EC4P 4EE

Set in 10/11 pt Sabon
by Columns of Reading
and printed in Great Britain
by Cox & Wyman Ltd
Reading, Berks

British Library Cataloguing in Publication Data
Bale, John, 1940–
    Geography in the primary school. –
    (Subjects in the primary school).
    1. Geography – Study and teaching
    (Elementary) – Great Britain
    I. Title   II. Series
    372.8'91044'0941   G76.5.G7

ISBN 0-7102-0792-1 (p)

Contents

Contents

Figures

Figures

Tables

Series Editor's Preface

After a decade of declining rolls, the number of children in primary schools is once again rising in most countries in the western world. The rise brings in its train an urgent demand for new teachers and ministries. School authorities and training institutions are turning to university graduates, offering one-year or other shortened courses rather than the conventional three- or four-year training course.

Such students know that they are keenly sought. Not only does the shortened course make them more immediately available to the schools, but also their expertise is highly appropriate to the widespread demand for real subject specialism to be available in the primary school curriculum.

But the translation of degree-level study into effective primary teaching is a difficult task – particularly in the short postgraduate course. This series is designed to help students to make the transition more readily. Each volume helps the reader to see the similarities between study at school and university and goes on, with advice, example and explanation, to show how subject knowledge can be structured and presented effectively in a primary school curriculum. Above all, the series aims to help beginning graduate teachers to transmit the enthusiasm that has led them to become specialists to new generations of young people.

John Eggleston

Introduction

> Waste of time is the leading feature of our present education.
> Not only are we taught a mass of rubbish, but what is not
> rubbish is taught so as to make us waste over it as much
> time as possible.
>
> Peter Kropotkin, 1913

Have things changed much since the radical Russian geographer,
Peter Kropotkin, wrote these words early in the present
century? Many would say that they have and that in primary
education in particular great strides have been made in the
present century bringing about substantial and progressive
changes. This book does not deny that such positive changes
have occurred. But in certain parts of the curriculum it can be
argued that there is little room for complacency. In the case of
geographical work in primary schools, for example, several
criticisms have been made in recent years. In 1974 a survey
undertaken by the Department of Education and Science (DES,
1974) revealed that of 215 primary schools sampled more than
61 per cent had 'poor schemes of work or no schemes at all'. In
addition, it has been established that teachers in British primary
schools do not use the local area enough: that visits into the
locality occur once per term or less for 82 per cent of primary
school teachers (Cracknell, 1976), and that 95 per cent
undertake local visits 'very rarely or never'. The same survey
revealed that 71 per cent of primary school teachers *never* used
large-scale maps with their pupils and that only 10 per cent
ever used case studies or sample studies.

The report of Her Majesty's Inspectorate, *Primary Education
in England*, (DES, 1978) gives equal cause for concern. The

1

report stressed a lack of progression and much superficiality and repetition in geographical work undertaken at the primary phase. In addition, much work undertaken was described as unexacting, while work on essential skills was poorly planned (see Catling, 1979).

Much geographical work in primary schools is undertaken within the framework of 'topic' work or some other form of integrated study. Cracknell (1976, 151), reporting a survey of geographical work in primary schools, noted that 'the topic or project is the most usual framework for geography teaching' in junior schools. In a survey by Bassey (1978) 68 per cent of teachers surveyed provided a curriculum activity on the primary school timetable called a 'topic' (only 7 per cent used the word 'project') whereas 'geography' featured for only 6 per cent. In middle schools 'geography' seems to appear for about 15 per cent, according to research by Connor (1976). However, the implicitly geographical nature of much topic work is confirmed by the titles of the most popular topics, 'Animals', 'Other Countries', 'Local Environment', 'Autumn' and 'Christmas' all being cited by 10 per cent or more in Bassey's survey.

Many primary schools remain unaware – usually through no fault of their own – of the exciting developments which have taken place in geography at all levels in recent years. What is more, the subject *is* recognised as important. In an address to the Geographical Association (the subject association of geography teachers) in 1985 Sir Keith Joseph, the then Secretary of State for Education, emphasised that 'geography has an important place in the primary as well as the secondary phase. It is capable of making an essential contribution from the beginning of the primary phase' (Joseph, 1985).

Over a decade ago Gould and White (1974) stressed that 'there are too many exciting and important concepts in the contemporary geographical viewpoint to eliminate them from the school curriculum so that children never become acquainted with them.' *A primary aim of this book is to alert teachers involved in the primary phase to some of these exciting ideas and ways in which they may be applied in the classroom.* Consider, for example, a class of busy 7- and 8-year-olds engaged in work on a project on a local park. They have identified from a large-scale map the kinds of buildings in the park, they have worked out the shortest routes across the park, identified different jobs done at different times of the year, surveyed the class to see the most popular uses to which the park is put, graphed the results and finally designed their own ideal park for themselves.

Another group of 10- and 11-year-old pupils is involved in field work which will lead to the preparation of a pamphlet on 'Our Locality'. Armed with maps and clipboards, they are noting and sketching items of the landscape which they think visitors to their local area would find interesting. When they return to school they plan to produce, with the aid of reference sources, a pamphlet consisting of maps and comments which they will distribute to parents and visitors at the school's summer fair.

These two vignettes typify the kind of geographical work which should be more widespread in our schools. In the pages which follow, we explore ways in which work of this type can be undertaken at the primary level. Before doing so, however, it will be worth considering what a distinctively *geographical* input to the school curriculum might look like. A common response of geographers to requests to outline the nature of their subject is to reply that geography is what geographers do! However, since at least Greek times those calling themselves geographers have tended to approach their subject from one of four perspectives. At different points in time different perspectives have been prominent and for this reason each perspective or tradition may be briefly reviewed.

Pattison (1964) considered that the four traditions of geography were the *human-environment* tradition, the *regional* tradition, the *earth-science* tradition and the *spatial* tradition. The nature of such swings in geographical thinking can be illustrated by comparing an elementary school textbook written at the turn of the present century with one written in the mid-1980s. The former would almost certainly exemplify the regional tradition of geography; indeed it might well illustrate the *worst* kind of regional geography in which the character and 'feeling' of places was totally lost and the subject was reduced to a gazetteer of locational facts. A present-day primary-school text, however, might well mirror the spatial tradition; it might focus on distributions, locations, patterns and relationships. The spatial tradition would permit the geographic study of everything from abacuses to zithers (Hill, 1972) since if something has a spatial distribution it becomes amenable to geographic study. At other points in time we might pick up geography textbooks which stressed the human-environment tradition. At worst these would be crudely environmentally deterministic, stressing the ways in which human abilities and behaviour are dependent on the physical environment; at best such a book would catch the symbiotic relationship between environment and humankind. The earth-science tradition might surface in a book designed to highlight the geomorphological, climatological or vegetational aspects of the earth's surface. What should be clear is that geography embraces a number of perspectives and is today far from synonymous with the place-name geography of yesteryear and it is to the discredit of the popular media that quiz shows tend to perpetuate an old-fashioned image of geography whenever 'geographical' questions are posed.

Although geography has rarely been able to justify itself as a discrete form of knowledge (Hirst, 1965; see also Graves, 1971), it can be justified as an approach to knowledge on at least three grounds. Firstly, no other subject area is consistently concerned with examining the character of *places* and the processes which led to that character. Secondly, geography is the only subject which adopts the *spatial* tradition alluded to earlier. Thirdly, geography is the only subject which focuses explicitly on the notion of *graphicacy*. This is the communication of spatial relationships by means other than literacy, numeracy and oracy (Boardman, 1983). Indeed, in a seminal paper, Balchin and Coleman (1965) referred to graphicacy as the 'fourth ace' in the educational pack, urging geography teachers through the widespread use of mapwork, to develop further this basic skill.

Everything that has been outlined so far is developed further in the pages which follow. The book commences by establishing what children know about the world before they ever enter a geography lesson. Initially, therefore, we focus on what children's private geographies are like. All children and all teachers possess such private geographies – worlds inside their heads, knowledge of which is gained by visits both real and vicarious. By the time they reach the early years of the junior school all children are, to greater or lesser degree, explorers, voyagers and map-makers; they are geographers without ever having been exposed to a geography lesson. It is an axiom of this book that it is upon these private geographies that the more formal geographical education should build, working from the known to the unknown. Such an old-fashioned educational tenet can be justified psychologically since for most of the primary-school years children are at a stage of intellectual development called the concrete operations stage (Piaget, 1955) in which they tend to think of actualities rather than possibilities, the latter coming at the formal operations stage in the years following primary education.

Because our concern in much of what follows is with the private worlds of individuals, it is important that we should know something not only about children's images of their worlds but also of their geographical behaviour. We therefore consider the geographies *of* young children and the ways they represent and perceive these geographies in the next chapter.

Chapter 2 briefly looks at the kinds of aims and objectives we might have for a primary school geographical education, focussing not only on the broad educational philosophies which different teachers might hold and the ways these viewpoints relate to geography, but also the more short-term objectives of deciding what to include in individual lessons or lesson units.

Having identified the mental maps which children possess in Chapter 1, we build upon these 'vernacular geographies' in Chapter 3 by considering the approaches we might adopt to the teaching of map skills and, in Chapter 4 to the way in which teachers might utilise the locality of the school and the neighbourhoods in which their pupils live.

Chapter 5 moves away from the immediate locality and considers problems and possibilities of dealing with more distant places in the geography classroom. In particular we raise the thorny problems of dealing with issues of stereotyping and racism. Chapter 6 is concerned with classroom strategies, ranging from chalk and talk to role-play. Modern geography teachers have to be adept at not only evaluating textbooks but also computer programs and for this reason a wide range of teaching approaches are examined. The book concludes with a look at the primary school geography curriculum and the way in which geographical work might be organised throughout the school. Tentative suggestions are provided about what children should know in certain areas at the completion of the primary phase.

Finding out about the forces, physical, social and economic, which bring about landscape change; mapping the world; finding the best place to locate a football club or a primary school; predicting the worst place to live in the event of a nuclear war or the best place to take a holiday; mapping levels of welfare. These are the kinds of questions which geographers ask of the world today. There is no reason why children between the ages of 7 and 11 should not be as excited by such problems as professors of geography. This book seeks to aid teachers in stimulating that excitement.

1

Young geographers and the worlds inside their heads

The images of the world which children (and adults) carry about inside their heads are derived, on the one hand, from personal experiences of visiting places and, on the other, from vicarious experiences *via* media of various kinds. This chapter is concerned with establishing the nature of children's geographical images upon which a geographical education might be constructed and the ways in which these images are represented. In order to understand the sources of these images we will also need to examine children's spatial behaviour and environmental experiences.

Children travel within their neighbourhoods reasonably frequently. They journey to more distant places less often, grasping and internalising *selective* images of these places. Such journeys would include visits to relatives, friends and holiday locations. Most geographical images, however, are projected by media such as radio, television, films, comics and books. As Pocock and Hudson (1978, 96) point out:

> depite modern mobility, man (sic) is still dependent to a
> considerable extent on secondary sources for his information
> of 'far places'. The cumulative influence of schooling and
> vicarious experiences through the arts and popular mass
> media enable him to know, and hold opinions about, many
> places never actually visited.

The variety of the information sources from which local, regional and national images are derived is shown in Figure 1.1. Children have reasonably detailed and accurate images of the personal spaces within which they regularly move (i.e. house and home); they possess somewhat less accurate images of

7

local places and much less accurate images of far places. It is these that are most frequently communicated *via* various media.

The geographical images we carry around with us are therefore the results of a *communication* process. The image is not only *produced* – sometimes carefully and with a desired end in view as in the case of propaganda – but also *projected*. It is then *received* as a mental map or geographical image. It will be up to the individual teacher, textbook writer, local educational authority or central government to decide if a subsequent stage is required, namely the *countering* of the image by presenting alternative regional or environmental information.

Later in this chapter we examine some aspects of the mental maps which children have of both local and distant places. However, before doing so it will be worth familiarising ourselves with various dimensions of the geographical behaviour of young people since it is important for teachers who wish to build upon children's own experiences of the world to appreciate their geographical activity and the ways in which it is influenced and constrained. It is to an initial appreciation of children's spatial behaviour, which in turn influences their private geographies, that we now turn.

Moving in the locality

In his detailed study of children's spatial behaviour, Roger Hart (1979) noted that for children aged 5 to 11 in a case study school in a small American town, three generalisations could be made concerning their local movements. The first of these was that the furthest distances children were allowed to go increased between the ages of 5 and 10 but not between 10 and 11. This applied to the distances children were allowed to go without having to ask or tell parents, the furthest they could go with parental permission, and the furthest with other children. Parentally restricted ranges of movement are derived from parents' fears about children's safety. Over time mobility increases, not only as a result of increased confidence and trust but also as a result of children's acquisition of simple vehicles such as bicycles.

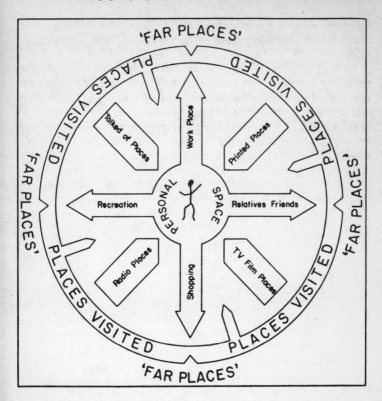

Figure 1.1 Sources of information, types of behaviour and environmental images
(Source: Goodey, 1971, 7)

A second general finding is that a number of environmental factors seem to influence children's spatial range. For example, Hart (1979, 72) found that children living in suburban areas tended to have a larger spatial range than children living in towns. One might extend this to suggest that the spatial range of rural children is greater than that of those living in urban environments. Good 'visual access', a quiet neighbourhood and a high proportion of children of similar age encourage relatively large amounts of spatial freedom.

A third finding of research into geographies of young

9

children is that significant gender-related differences exist in their spatial behaviour. Hart's work revealed that whereas the main maximum distance of 'range with permission' of girls of 9 to 11 years was 860 metres, that for boys was 1002 metres. More dramatic differences were found for younger children, boys of between 5 and 8 years of age having a mean maximum distance of more than twice that of girls. Similar, though slightly less dramatic, results were found for English primary school children in the city of Coventry (Matthews, 1984, 330) (Table 1.1).

Table 1.1   Distances of furthest point from home: boys and girls

Grades/age	Mean of distances of furthest point from home (metres)	
	Boys	Girls
grade 1–3[a]	244	114
grade 4–6[a]	684	283
age 6[b]	184	177
age 7[b]	272	265
age 8[b]	217	210
age 9[b]	599	393
age 10[b]	613	401
age 11[b]	1061	680

(Based on (a) Hart, 1979, 47 and (b) Matthews, 1984, 330)

Such differences are confirmed by Newson and Newson (1968), whose study of 4-year-olds in Nottingham revealed similar results. Their conclusion is that the restricted geographical range of girls results from greater parental fear of molestation than with boys. As the Newsons (1978, 108) observed from a study of 7-year-olds.

> by the age of 7, and in a whole variety of ways, the daily experience of little boys in towns of where they are allowed to go, how they spend their time and to what extent they are kept under surveillance is already markedly different from that of little girls.

As a result of such differences in mobility boys tend to show 'an awareness of places further away from their homes than

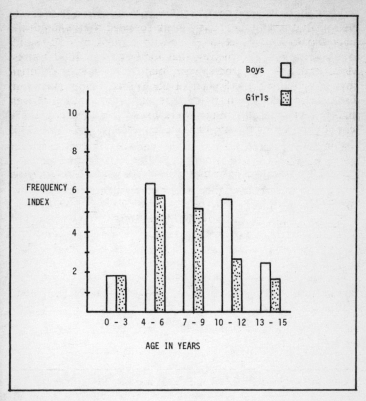

Figure 1.2 Frequency index of children's outdoor activities in Plankan, Stockholm
(Source: Björklid, 1982, 124)

girls' (Matthews, 1984, 329) though the precise information boys and girls have about the places they visit may not vary significantly. Girls *are* expected to spend more time indoors and help their mothers about the house. Playing in fields, climbing trees and generally being outdoors is considered more appropriate for boys. A study of children on a Stockholm housing estate (Björklid, 1982) showed that girls spent substantially less time than boys in outdoor activities, the differences being greatest between the ages of 4 and 12 (Figure 1.2).

As Hart (1979, 66) stresses, 'there is no biological basis for such different behaviors'. Such gender differences are given

11

emphasis here because they *may* contribute partially towards the subsequent underachievement by girls in map-reading tests, a subject we return to later.

Common factors influencing the primary school child's spatial behaviour can be summarised in the form of a map (Figure 1.3). It is the immediate locality which the child first explores and which provides stimuli for further exploration and discovery. The locality generates powerful images which reside well into maturity. But within the locality place preferences will emerge. Fields, trees, ponds, playgrounds and streets free from traffic are all places about which children will discover detailed knowledge. On the other hand, dangerous places like quarries, rivers, and motorways, and 'scary' places like woods and old houses, are avoided.

The teacher needs to be aware of the spatial characteristics of children's behaviour because it is upon these foundations, and upon the mental images which they generate, that more formal geographical education will be built. We have looked briefly at the nature of children's geographical behaviour. Having done so, we can now proceed to an examination of how they *represent* the world inside their heads.

Representing the locality

Children represent the area most familiar to them as cognitive maps. From birth to about 2 years of age children's understanding of their environment is entirely egocentric. Piaget and his associates (Piaget and Inhelder, 1956, Piaget *et al.*, 1960) have shown that by the age of about 4 children are beginning to understand the location of objects around them in a topological sense, i.e. in relation to one another. In the infants school children usually view their environment as a series of links and nodes and come to represent this cartographically as a topological cognitive map (Catling, 1978b). This link-picture map is still highly egocentric, with well-known places such as the school or the homes of friends shown as 'pictures', all connected to the home. Direction, orientation, and scale are non-existent on such maps (Figure 1.4a).

Link-picture maps evolve into quasi-egocentric picture maps in which the degree of connectivity between known places is

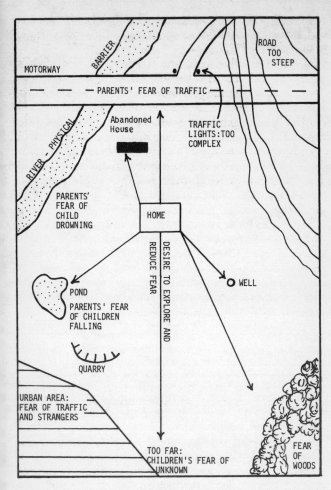

Figure 1.3   Common forces influencing children's spatial behaviour (Based on Hart, 1979)

increased. Refinements exist in so far as roads may be in plan form, but buildings remain iconic in representation. Scale and direction continue to be inaccurate. By the age of 7 children usually reach a stage of development in which their topological representation of the world becomes 'projective', i.e. three-dimensional objects such as buildings become represented two-

13

Figure 1.4   Stages in cognitive mapping. The quasi-egocentric and quasi-projective stages occur between the two stages shown
(a) *above left*   Topological (egocentric) stage. A link-picture map of the village of Betley, Staffs, drawn by a boy of 5 years of age. Known places (countryside, bottom left, shops, top) are connected to home. Direction, scale, orientation and distance are non-existent. The street, drawn in plan form, is rather untypical of this stage
(b) *above right*   Euclidean (abstract) stage. This accurate and detailed map of the village drawn by the same child at the age of 10 illustrates an abstractly co-ordinated and hierarchically integrated map. Scale, direction and symbolic representation are well developed

dimensionally (Boardman, 1983). By this age children are able to represent their localities as quasi-maps, possessing more detail, better co-ordination and continuity of routes. Direction, orientation, distance and scale are all improved and some buildings will be in plan form.

The average 11-year-old child will be able to construct a 'true map' of his or her environment without being formally taught to do so. By this age children will have progressed from the egocentric to the abstract stage and will have constructed, abstractly, co-ordinated and hierarchically integrated maps. Because symbols are no longer depicted iconically, a key will be required.

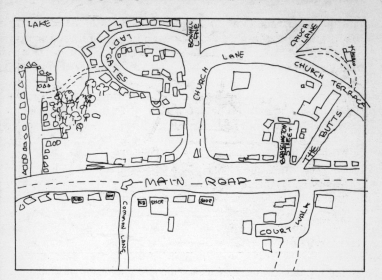

So far cartographic skill has been considered as the ability to represent the locality. This is not, of course, in any way synonymous with map *reading*. Usually map reading is taught in the junior school from the ages of 7 or 8 and approaches to teaching the elements of mapwork are considered in the next chapter. However, evidence (Blaut and Stea, 1974; Blades and Spencer, 1986) suggests that the untaught ability to read a map does exist in children as young as 3. It therefore seems that children may actually be able to read simple maps before they can read simple words. For example, using very simple large-scale maps (scale 1:50) with 3-year-old children suggested that they could push a toy car through a layout, following the route which had been marked on a map of the layout (Blades and Spencer, 1986). As Catling (1979) stresses, the study of map ability in pre-school children is valuable because it shows children's potential in practical geographical situations. It demonstrates that very young children learn by doing, an old-fashioned educational tenet, but one which needs to be continually borne in mind when considering map work with children in the junior school.

So far we have concentrated only on the way in which age

15

affects cartographic ability and representation. Three other important variables need to be taken into account also, namely race, sex and class. The question of what is meant by race is alluded to later, but at this stage we can consider the way in which a black child called Dave, in Boston, Massachusetts, drew a map of his home area. Dave's map (Figure 1.5) shows a considerable amount of detail north of Parker Street and a large, relatively blank area to the south.

It emerged from research by Ladd (1967) that this area to the south was where whites lived and that Dave was physically afraid of visiting it. Other black children represented Parker Street as being disproportionately wide, reflecting the physical, cultural, and racial gulf which it represented to them. Many black children had never ventured across this street and were therefore unable to depict anything but *terra incognita* on their mental map.

Just as the maps of different ethnic groups reflect their different spatial behaviour, so too may the maps of boys and girls. It is widely acknowledged that differences exist in spatial abilities, though whether the observed underachievement of girls and women in spatial tests is innate or culturally derived is the subject of considerable debate. Some argue that neurological factors unique to girls affect their spatial ability, hence contributing to an explanation of their relatively poorer performance than boys in map-reading tests (e.g. Boardman and Towner, 1979). This underachievement is illustrated by the work of Matthews (1986), working with primary school children in Coventry. Given freehand maps to draw of their localities, Matthews (1986, 125) stressed that 'by the age of seven some boys had already drawn plan maps, a skill which girls generally had not acquired until 10 years of age. Similarly a higher proportion of boys achieved the ability to represent places in a coherent and organised manner by the age of 11'.

However, many observers argue that girls are held back by cultural factors, their more housebound and spatially restricted behaviour and the nature of their childhood toys (girls tend to have less access to 'map-like' toys like train sets) inhibiting their spatial development. But as Mazey and Lee (1983, 49) point out, 'the innate differences which women *might* possess can be reduced or eliminated through education and training programs designed to develop spatial skills'.

16

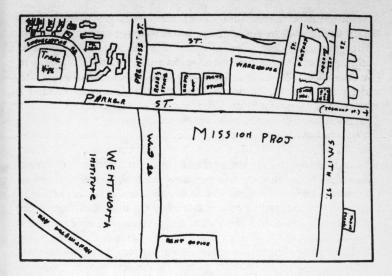

Figure 1.5   A black child's map of part of Boston, USA. The area to
the south of Parker Street is occupied by whites
(Source: Ladd, 1967)

The subject of class differences in educational performance
has attracted a vast literature, though virtually nothing exists
which refers to class differences in geographical achievement at
the primary level. We can extrapolate from existing findings,
however, and infer that middle-class children will tend to out-
perform those from working-class backgrounds as a result of
the nature of domestic stimuli to which they are exposed.
Maps, atlases and other 'educational' media are more likely to
be found in middle-class than working-class homes. Such media
are legitimated as being valuable in a formal educational sense
and it would be hardly surprising that, if asked to undertake
mapping activities, those from middle-class backgrounds
tended to achieve better results. However, work by Wilson
(1981, 157) in Australia revealed that socio-economic status,
while related to 'map reasoning development' was not a good
indicator or predictor of such ability in children of primary age.
Work in Glasgow by Jahoda (1963), on the other hand,
indicated that children aged 6–11 from middle-class schools

17

consistently outscored those from working-class schools in tests designed to show their conceptualisation of the nature of Glasgow and its relationship with Scotland and Britain. For example, of children from the middle-class schools only 7 per cent had no clear ideas of Glasgow as an entity whereas the respective figure for the working-class schools was 29 per cent.

Knowledge of distant places

As we move away from the immediate locality children's knowledge of the world becomes inevitably blurred. They become more dependent on secondary rather than personal sources of contact with places. Radio, film and television powerfully influence children's images of places, as do the books and comics which they read. The knowledge which we have of all places can be measured on two basic indicators, quantity and quality. Let us first consider the *quantity* of information which children possess of places beyond their immediate environment.

Drawing on the work of Peter Gould (1972), we can review the impact of age and distance on the amount of information which children have about distant places. Working in the city of Jönköping in Sweden, Gould asked children of 7, 9, 11 and 13 years of age to write down in a specified time period the names of all the places in Sweden which they could think of. For each age group the aggregate information was carto-graphically represented as an 'information surface'. For the youngest groups the most frequently named places were either near Jönköping itself (a kind of neighbourhood effect) or near Sweden's biggest cities – Stockholm and Malmö. As the children got older the neighbourhood effect intensified and other large cities like Göteborg and Umeå were mentioned. So too was northern Sweden, an anomaly Gould suggests, resulting from a newsworthy miners' strike in the iron-ore fields at the time of his survey (Figure 1.6).

However, it is not just the size of the places or the distance from home or the newsworthiness of it which disposes children to have knowledge of it. A place may be near to home physically but at a considerable cultural distance away from where we live. The intra-urban maps of Boston's black children

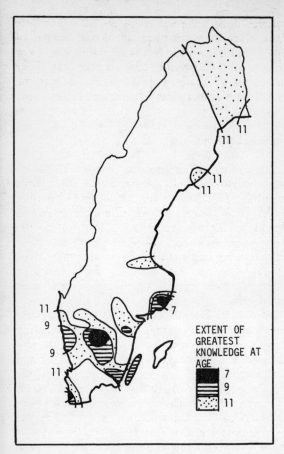

Figure 1.6 Information surfaces of primary school
children from Jönköping, Sweden
(Based on Gould, 1972)

have already illustrated this. At the international scale boundaries between countries act as barriers to the flow of information and we can draw on more of Gould's work in Scandinavia to illustrate this point. Children at Ed in Sweden and at nearby Halden in Norway undertook a similar exercise to those from Jönköping whose geographical knowledge was described above. The children in Ed could recall many places in

19

Figure 1.7   Information fields for children living at (a) Ed in Sweden
and (b) Halden in Norway
(Source: Gould and White, 1974)

Sweden but few in Norway; the opposite was the case for the
Norwegian children.

'Clearly the boundary has a severe effect upon the flows of
information to children only a few miles apart in geographic
space' (Gould and White, 1974, 146) (Figure 1.7). Such studies
bear replication in other countries but their outcome seems

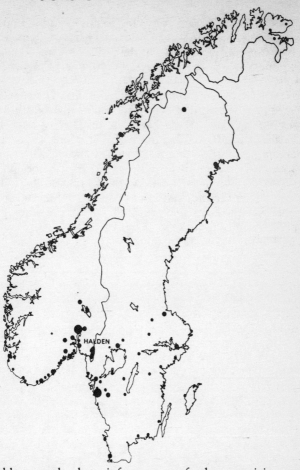

predictable, namely the reinforcement of ethnocentricism and us-and-them-ism.

The reasons for such geographical patterns should be obvious. Not only do children travel to more places near home than far away, but the media also bias their coverage in favour of local, as opposed to distant, places. Such bias can be illustrated by the coverage afforded different nations of the world in a newspaper published in Nigeria. Figure 1.8 clearly shows the world in 'Nigerian newspaper space'; Nigeria itself and Africa are given substantial coverage whereas the Americas,

21

Europe and Asia are tiny in terms of the amounts of information provided for Nigerian readers. Similar maps, drawn from the perspective of the BBC News and *Pravda*, have been drawn by Cole and Whysall (1968) and show predictable results.

Places clearly vary in their media visibility. Owen and Mason (1980) have shown that the most 'visible' non-North American cities in the *New York Times* in the 1970s were London, Moscow and Paris. The most visible countries were USSR, Vietnam and Great Britain. Obviously the media 'visibility' of places will change over time, some places becoming less newsworthy and therefore less visible as times change. Teachers can build on the motivation provided by 'visible' places (such as the Olympic Games, World Cup, etc.) in the development of topic and project work (see Chapter 5).

In addition to these quantitative differences in the informa-

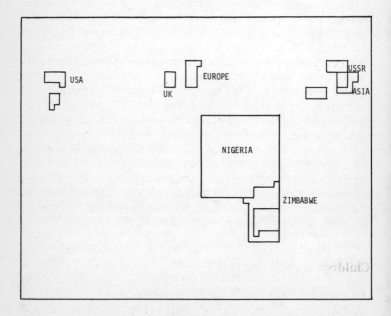

Figure 1.8 Areas of the world drawn proportional to the number of mentions received in a Nigerian newspaper during a period of one month

tion provided about places teachers need to be fully aware of the *qualitative* variations which also exist in the input of information about the world which our children receive. The quality of information about places poses problems for teachers, since it may lead to them having to counter simple factual errors on the one hand but racism on the other. Some examples of each of these kinds of problems can be illustrated in turn.

Factual errors are difficult to avoid if one is not fully versed in the subject or topic being taught; they are even more difficult to avoid if one has no control over the media to which children are exposed. Consider the case of a comic-strip presentation of a story set in the Falkland Islands (Malvinas) and published in the *Girl Annual 1962*, brought to the attention of readers of the *Guardian* 'Diary' at the time of the Falklands/Malvinas War. In the comic in question the white-skinned heroine, Isabel, is shown arriving in Stanley, capital of the Falklands, surrounded by a throng of *black* faces. One native Falklander (depicted in a turban) says, 'A white woman!'; another, 'Isn't she lovely!'. Isabel asks, 'Why is everyone interested in me?' 'It's because you're the first white woman they've ever seen,' replies a humble Falkland Islander.

Such inaccuracy is so blatant that most (hopefully all) teachers would instantly recognise it and counter it by providing more accurate information about the geographical context of the story. Often, however, misinformation is more subtly projected; boys' comics in particular continue to extol the glory of wartime victories against erstwhile enemies, hence predisposing readers towards particular peoples and particular nations. Teachers may themselves unintentionally pass on misinformation about places to their children and we consider this next in our discussion of stereotyping.

Children's world images

As a result of the media inputs they have received, children's mental maps of the world tend to be stereotypical and ethnocentric. A stereotype is commonly defined as 'an image containing distorted or erroneous information' (Burgess, 1974, 167), although it is acknowledged that the discrediting or

23

substantiation of stereotypes can be difficult since some kind of objective data are needed against which stereotypes can be compared. However, considerable evidence does exist to show that children's images of places contain highly selective information and are therefore erroneous.

An example can be provided from the results of a word-association test undertaken with primary school children of 8 and 9 years of age from Wokingham in England. The test revealed that the most frequently cited responses to 'Africa' were 'lions', 'heat', 'snakes', 'elephants', 'trees' and 'tigers' (Table 1.2).

Table 1.2   Images of Africa

Item	Number of mentions	Item	Number of mentions
Lion	19	Animals	10
Heat	14	Jungle	9
Snakes	14	Monkey	8
Elephant	13	Desert	8
Forest, trees	13	Grassland	8
Tigers	12	Sun	7
Palm trees	12	nuts, coconuts	7
black people	12	Bananas	7
natives	10	Islands	7

(Source: Storm, 1984, 65)

Should we be satisfied with such images? Clearly, there is a tendency for children to associate Africa with the exotic. There is no mention of poverty, exploitation, racism, cities, oil, apartheid, and numerous other *possible* images which they *could* have received.

Young children's *attitudes* towards different nationalities tend to change over time. Unless children are exposed to constant adverse comments at home, they generally tend to display 'a marked rise in favourable attitudes' (Carnie, 1972, 126) towards peoples of other nationalities. There is a tendency for young children to view relationships between particular nations as being more hostile than is the case for older juniors (Carnie, 1972, 110). The 7-year-old is more likely to think in

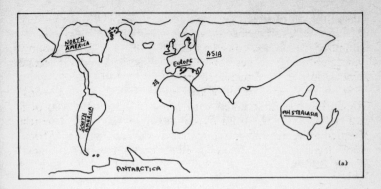

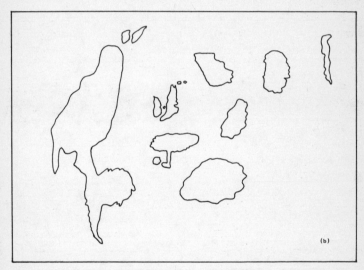

Figure 1.9 Freehand sketch maps of the world drawn by two 10-year-old pupils. Both pupils came from middle-class homes and were regarded as being above average in general ability

terms of absolutes (e.g. good – bad) whereas the 11-year-old begins to see shades of relationships. Some have suggested that a peaking of favourable attitudes comes at around the age of 10, but others feel that it is somewhat later. However, whatever the precise age there seems little doubt that 'in the primary

25

school the study of places should certainly take account of younger children's curiosity and relative openness' (ILEA, 1981, 5) with respect to other nations and nationalities.

In terms of representing the world cartographically, it is quite possible for some children aged 10 or 11 to draw remarkably accurate freehand maps of the world from memory. For a given age group, however, the degree of accuracy of maps drawn by individuals is likely to vary tremendously (Figure 1.9). Children from homes lacking an atlas are obviously going to be at a disadvantage in this respect and for such children it is not uncommon for them to be unable to distinguish land from sea when presented with a world map.

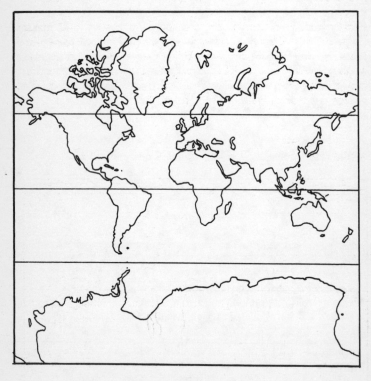

Figure 1.10 Map projections producing different shaped worlds: (a) the Mercator projection, which distorts area;

Children's world maps tend to be ethnocentric in the sense that if drawn by British pupils Britain will tend to be central and more distant places drawn less accurately in terms of shape. The relative crudity of the shape of east Asia and Australia in Figure 1.9 is exemplary. It is possible that the way in which children visualise the outlines of the world's land masses is influenced strongly by the pervasiveness of the Mercator projection, still commonly used in the early pages of atlases and in other media. The well-known effect of this projection is to exaggerate the size of land masses towards the poles and understate the relative size of land areas in the tropics. For this reason considerable pressure (e.g. Gill, 1984) has recently been exerted for greater use (as wall maps in primary-school classrooms, for example) of the Peters projection, which more accurately depicts the areas of land masses (Figure 1.10). This projection is advocated by both the United Nations and Christian Aid. While representing area more accurately, it does distort shape and as a result the debate continues about which map projection should be best used to depict the world (Bain, 1984; Storm, 1986).

(b) the Peters projection, which distorts shape

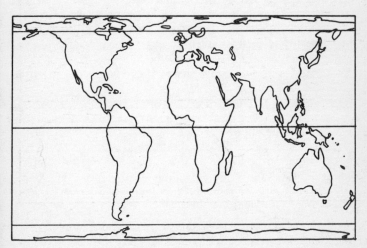

Racism in geography

We have already referred to the stereotypical images which children hold of particular peoples and places. We have suggested that for most of the time this is the result of simple bias and ignorance. However, others would argue that among the subjects on the school curriculum geography is as guilty as any, and more guilty than some, of instilling racist attitudes among our pupils. Among the first to emphasise the racist nature of school geography was the radical American geographer, William Bunge (1965), who stressed that the language, coverage and attitudes projected by the subject justified the label 'racist'. The Rampton Report (Rampton, 1981) described racism as a

> set of attitudes and behaviour towards people of another race which is based on the belief that races are distinct and can be graded as 'superior' and 'inferior'. A racist is therefore someone who believes that people of a particular colour or national origin are inherently inferior, so that their identity, culture, self-esteem, views and feelings are of less value than his or her own and can be disregarded or treated as less important.

The inferiority of people from countries other than our own is implicitly communicated by a vast range of media including comics, films, television programmes, books and newspapers. Gill (1983) has suggested that state racism is implicit in successive immigration legislation, the 'over-policing' of inner urban areas housing large numbers of black people, and in the Nationality Act.

The problem of accusations of racism is that what is racist to some critics is merely conservatism to others. It is certainly possible for teachers who would regard themselves as liberals to be accused of racism by certain radicals. For this reason it is of importance to be aware of the *ideological* nature of much content and discourse in education and we return to this problem later. For the moment, however, consider the following examples of what Milner (1975, 232) considers to be examples of implicit racism. In a book titled *Our Neighbours and their Work for Us*, the following description refers to the West Indies:

> The heat of the sun makes the work of growing sugar too hard for white people. Even the natives on the plantations work in very light clothes.

In *Work in Other Lands* we are told that in Sri Lanka:

> each of the plantations where the tea is grown and picked and packed is looked after by a white man . . . he sees that all the people who work on his plantation work well and honestly.

Such quotations are taken from textbooks published first in the 1930s but still being used as late as the 1960s. Since then things have not changed very significantly. Jingoism, ethnocentricism and the decontroversialising of highly controversial events in world (and local) geography continue to pervade much of the curriculum. One recently published textbook, for example, compared a white-faced, suited 'city gent' described as 'civilised' with an unclad black plainsman described as 'primitive'. Such vocabulary begs many questions, among the most important being the kinds of connotations certain words carry with them. Another well-known text contains a map entitled 'The World's Problem Regions'; these regions are found to be in places like Amazonia, the Kalahari, Greenland and central Australia. *For whom* are these said to be environmentally problematic? Certainly not for the indigenous populations who lived there for thousands of years in equilibrium with their environment and in generally egalitarian societies. The main problems for such peoples have come not from the physical environment but from the relatively recent invasion of their lands by Europeans.

In some cases misinformation can be presented through sheer ignorance of place knowledge. An annotated and beautifully drawn map of Iceland on one primary classroom wall included labels such as 'polar bears' and 'eskimoes'. Imaginative teaching perhaps, but the teaching of nonsense. Similarly headteachers have been overheard to call Africa a 'country', a simple error but one that is then passed on to their pupils. We all too often pass on our own biases to our pupils. Consider the statement overheard in a lesson on 'settlement' (would 'colonisation' or 'conquest' have been a more appropriate word?) of North America by Europeans: 'When they arrived the Europeans had trouble with the Indians.' Rarely is it suggested that the indigenous Americans encountered certain problems when Europeans invaded their nations!

What worlds do we want for them?

Much of this chapter has focussed on children's views of the world, both local and distant. We have considered also the way children come to represent the world, both cartographically and verbally and have noted some of the factors which influence the way they represent both local and distant environments. This approach has been adopted for two reasons. First, it is an axiom of this book that it is from the worlds inside children's heads that school geography should build. As early as 1926 James Fairgreave was arguing for geography teachers to work from the known to the unknown, from the particular to the general and from the concrete to the abstract (Naish, 1982, 29). It is important to follow Fairgreave's advice at the primary school level and this clearly involves utilising children's own views of the world.

A second reason for focussing on children's private geographies, their untutored or vernacular world views, is to ask whether we are satisfied with such perspectives. Are we happy with the limited map ability of many of our children? Are we content with the stereotyped and blinkered view of the world many pupils possess? Do we want to turn out passive young people who have not begun to question conventional wisdoms? If the answer to each of these questions is 'yes', there is little point in reading further. If on the other hand the reader is interested in exploring ways of teaching geography to young people, by geographers – a situation which recent government pronouncements have endorsed – then we will need to begin to consider what our aims and objectives are in a geographical education, a subject we turn to in the next chapter.

Further reading

Roger Hart, *Children's Experience of Place*, Irvington, New York, 1979.

Hugh Matthews, 'Cognitive mapping abilities of young boys and girls', *Geography*, 69, 4, 1984, 327–36.

D. Milner, *Children and Race*, Penguin, Harmondsworth, 1975.

2

Aims and objectives

This chapter serves to briefly examine both general aims and more specific objectives of geographical education in primary schools.

As well as instruction in specifically geographical education (e.g. the learning of map skills, place names, processes, etc.) geography may serve to aid instruction in a large number of areas of learning and experience (e.g. aesthetic, mathematical). The broad aims of education may also be well served by geography. Walford (1981a) has suggested that four possible broad educational philosophies may exist, though no single teacher is likely to adhere rigidly to any one of these. Nevertheless the classification is helpful though it needs to be stressed that it is what a sociologist might term an 'ideal type model' and not meant to reflect any set of viewpoints held by any sets of people.

A teacher, Walford suggests, might hold one of the following 'base positions' in terms of educational philosophy, utilitarian, liberal, child-centred or reconstructionist. Each may be briefly alluded to in turn.

Utilitarian primary-school geography teachers will see it as their job to prepare pupils to survive in the world outside, and beyond, the primary school. There will therefore be a strong emphasis on a curriculum and a teaching style geared towards the inculcation of skills and knowledge which might be setting children on the road towards getting a job. It has been implicit in much writing in the recent 'Industry Year 1986' that primary school children should be introduced to aspects of industry in modern Britain with a view towards inculcating positive attitudes towards industry at an early age. Information, skills and the basics of geography would be the objectives of a teacher adopting this position.

Liberal education in geography at the primary level would focus more on turning out 'little geographers' at the end of their days at this level of education. By this is meant that by the age of 11 pupils would be able to view the world through the spectacles of the geographer. Teachers would monitor carefully the subject's conceptual and methodological changes which would then be adapted and adopted at the primary level, in much the style of Cole and Beynon's *New Ways in Geography* (1969). Games and simulations rather than didactic modes of teaching might also typify the liberal educator, willing to take on board new developments as they occur.

Child-centred 'geographers who have been influenced by this tradition do not, in all probability, care very much whether they are geographers or not. They would see their role primarily as an educator of the whole person, breaking down the artificial barriers of "subjects" and integrating experience wherever possible' (Walford, 1981a, 219). Project and topic work would typify such teachers' work. Subjectivity in experiencing the environment, sensory walks, 'feeling' towards places and environments and other experiential approaches would characterise the child-centred geography teacher. This approach to teaching has been particularly associated with the British primary school in the post-war period.

Reconstructionist geographical education is concerned with changing society and hence engendering 'a kind of divine discontent' (Walford, 1981a, 220) in the pupil. The teacher espousing this viewpoint will encourage the child to challenge the status quo, to ask penetrating questions, to establish informal learning networks with people outside the school itself. Geographically, ideas of spatial injustice, pollution and the distribution of power and its effects on society (to name but a few ideas) would be stressed.

It is probable that we all hold elements of each of these basic philosophical positions. Within these broad positions more specific short-term objectives nevertheless need to be identified. Teachers ultimately face the task of asking what their objectives will be in geography this term, this week, tomorrow. . . . Two broad domains (Bloom *et al.*, 1956) within which objectives

Table 2.1 Objectives for geography in the early years (5–8)

The curriculum for the early years should help pupils to:

1 extend their awareness of their surroundings;
2 identify and explore features of the local environment;
3 distinguish between the variety of ways in which land is used and the variety of purposes for which buildings are constructed;
4 recognise and investigate changes taking place in the local area;
5 gain some understanding of the different contributions which a variety of individuals and services make to the life of the local community;
6 relate different types of human activity to specific places within the local area;
7 develop an awareness of cultural and ethnic diversity within our society, whilst recognising the similar activities, interests and aspirations of different people;
8 extend their vocabulary and develop concepts which enable them to describe the relative position and spatial attributes of features within their environment;
9 understand some of the ways in which the local environment affects people's lives;
10 develop an awareness of seasonal changes of weather and of the effects which weather conditions have on the growth of plants, on the lives of animals and on their own and other people's activities;
11 begin to develop an interest in people and places beyond their immediate experience;
12 observe accurately and develop simple skills of enquiry;
13 extend and refine their vocabulary and develop language skills;
14 develop mathematical concepts and number skills;
15 develop their competence to communicate in a variety of forms, including pictures, drawings and simple diagrams and maps.

(Source: Bennetts, 1985)

may be structured can be identified. These are the cognitive and affective domains.

The *cognitive domain* is essentially concerned with categorising different kinds of knowledge and skills. Immediately we are led to question the balance between skills and knowledge; how many place names should young children know? What map skills should they possess at the age of 11? Should they be able to comprehend certain geographical ideas at the age of 9?

In terms of geographical knowledge no definitive checklist exists which states what children should know at different age levels. In the final chapter of this book we make some tentative suggestions about this kind of problem. But the learning of factual information is only part of the cognitive domain. Comprehension, extrapolation and synthesising are skills which will be taught in various contexts in geography. In the area of comprehension, map-reading and other areas of graphicacy loom large. Again, we refer to these kinds of skills and what we might reasonably expect primary school pupils to have achieved in Chapter 7.

More specific objectives for primary-school geography have recently been outlined by Bennetts (1985, 304) for the early (Table 2.1) and the late (Table 2.2) years of the primary phase. The content of these tables is authoritative, helpful and comprehensive, whether geography is a separate part of the timetable or not.

It will be noted that in Table 2.2 considerable emphasis is placed on the *local* environment, reinforcing the points made earlier. However, the content of each table raises a number of questions. For example, in Table 2.1 it is suggested that children explore features of their local environment. But *which* features are not made clear. Consider also the suggestion that young children should understand some of the ways in which the local environment affects people's lives. Does this mean the *physical* or the *political* environment – or both? We are clearly on safer ground with the final part of Table 2.1, which advocates the development of cartographic communication.

Likewise, in Table 2.2 there are problems with the objective (7) which focuses on the identification of cities and countries. How many of these should the child be expected to recognise? Is there a threshold size below which it is not necessary to know, from memory, the name of a particular country? To a large extent the individual teacher will be left to decide the answers to such questions and in some cases a teacher's personal educational philosophy will influence the interpretation placed on such objectives. We return to some of these considerations in subsequent chapters and in the final chapter when we look at some aspects of the primary geography curriculum.

Table 2.2 Objectives for geography in the later years of primary (8–11)

The curriculum for the later years of primary should help pupils to:

1 investigate at first-hand features of their local environment: its weather; its surface features; and some of the activities of its inhabitants, especially those aspects that involve spatial and environmental relationships;

2 study some aspects of life and conditions in a number of other small areas in Britain and abroad, which provide comparisons with their own locality. From such studies pupils should gain knowledge and understanding of some of the ways in which people have used, modified and cared for their surroundings, and of the influence of environmental conditions, culture and technology on the activities and ways of life of the present inhabitants;

3 gain some appreciation of the importance of location in human affairs and some understanding of such concepts as distance, direction, spatial distribution and spatial links (especially the movements of people and goods between places), having applied these ideas in appropriate contexts;

4 have some understanding of changes taking place in their own locality and in other areas studied, including some appreciation of the ways in which human decisions influence these changes;

5 develop an appreciation of the variety of life styles in Britain and abroad, which reflect a variety of cultures, and develop positive attitudes towards different communities and societies;

6 become acquainted with a variety of maps, including large-scale maps of their own neighbourhood and be able to apply simple techniques of map reading and interpretation;

7 acquire familiarity with globes and with atlas maps and be able to identify such features as the continents and oceans, countries, cities, highland and lowland, coasts and rivers;

8 a. carrying out observations and in collecting, organising and recording information as part of an enquiry;
   b. using a variety of sources of information about their own locality and other places;

Table 2.2 *continued*

  c. communicating their findings and ideas, with varying degres of
     precision, in writing, pictures, models, diagrams and maps;
9 continue to develop language and mathematical skills through
  studies in geography;
10 appreciate the significance of people's attitudes and values in the
   context of particular environmental or social issues which they
   have investigated.

(Source: Bennetts, 1985)

Bloom's second set of objectives, in the *affective* domain, is concerned with the learning of values and attitudes. This is a less easily assessed area of geography teaching because it is less easy to establish whether we have taught a child an attitude than a fact. However, we might expect attitudes to have changed if behaviour changes. In the affective domain Bloom is not concerned with explicitly political or religious attitudes and values. Rather, the attitudes we are concerned with here are things like attending, questioning and valuing. An aim of all teachers, presumably, will be to have an attentive class. Many will also want an enquiring class. However, in some cases teachers may be involved in changing social behaviour outside school as a result of attitudes taught in the classroom. The work of health educators and their desire to change children's attitudes towards smoking and other drug taking comes immediately to mind. In a more geographical context, many teachers advocate the teaching of anti-racist attitudes in the classroom – a view also stressed by the Geographical Association (Walford, 1985). The *kind* of geography curriculum teachers adopt will obviously influence children's abilities in both the cognitive and the affective domain.

Confluent geographical education. Of course, affective and cognitive domains should not be thought of as being totally separated. It can be argued that the two are inextricably intermeshed. For example, cognitive learning (of, for example, facts and skills) may be made easier if affective learning (of, for example, interest and involvement) has been achieved. In addition, affective objectives such as the learning of empathy can be included, along with more cognitive objectives. The integration of cognitive and affective domains in the context of a given topic is known as *confluent education*.

Consider, for example, a class of 10- or 11-year-olds working on a topic on 'Forests'. Assume that the teacher wishes to have children understand that many forested areas of the world are threatened with destruction and that Amazonia is taken as a case study. The teacher may wish to stress the search for mineral wealth, the development of new agricultural settlements and the penetration of the trans-Amazonia highway. All these will be part of the cognitive domain, shown on the left-hand side of Figure 2.1. However, a confluence with the affective domain is brought about by having children consider the feelings of the people involved. For example, we might focus on the indigenous peoples of the Amazon rain forest and consider their views of events. We may extrapolate from their experiences and relate them to how *we* might feel in situations in which we appear helpless. This area of education is shown on the right-hand side of Figure 2.1. Confluent education emphasises the integration of both knowledge and experience, of academic and private geographies. 'It has as its goal the

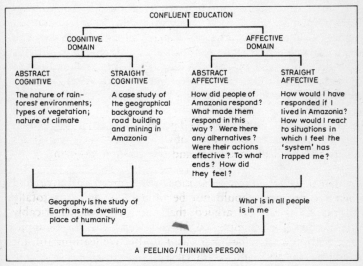

Figure 2.1   Confluent education applied to a geographical example (Based on an idea by Fien, 1983)

education of a *feeling-thinking* person, not one in whom either aspect of the mind is ignored' (Fien, 1983, 49).

In thinking about how we might organise our aims and objectives for geography teaching we might employ a simple model based on ideas developed by Kemp (1971). Having decided what we want our children to learn, we decide on the subject content required to achieve these objectives. We then design teaching and learning activities and decide on appropriate resources. Having taught the lesson, or series of lessons, in which we hope to achieve our objectives, we undertake some kind of evaluation to discover if we have been successful or not. Should we discover that our objectives have not been achieved and that the children have clearly failed to respond to our teaching strategies we employ a feedback process to reconsider or revise our objectives, content or strategies. This sequence is shown in Figure 2.2.

This is a very *general* model and teachers may wish to incude certain modifications. For example, it might be desirable to include a 'pre-test' before the teaching stage in order to

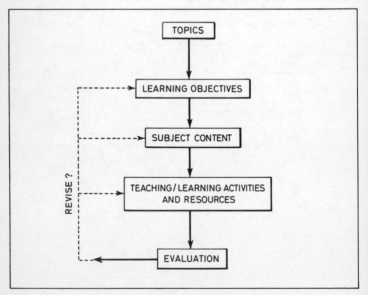

Figure 2.2   An objectives model of curriculum development

establish whether the pupils will be capable of the work we are planning for them. A more precise consideration of subject content and the wide variety of teaching strategies available for the individual teacher forms the subject of subsequent chapters.

Conclusion. The educational aims of primary school geography teachers will depend in large part on their deep-seated philosophical positions. The general objectives may be to fit children into the world of work on the one hand or change society on the other. Most teachers probably possess elements of a number of basic philosophical standpoints. Objectives in geography will be both cognitive, concerned with the acquisition of facts and skills, and affective, concerned with learning attitudes. In the chapters which follow we explore ways in which different kinds of teaching strategies seek to satisfy our aims and objectives.

Further reading

Trevor Bennetts, Geography from 5 to 16; a view from the inspectorate, *Geography*, 70, 4, 1985, 299–314.

Rex Walford, *Signposts for Geography Teaching*, Longman, London, 1981.

Department of Education and Science, *Geography from 5 to 16*, Curriculum Matters 7, HMSO, London, 1986.

3

Teaching map skills

There is little controversy surrounding the assertion that all primary school children should be introduced to map work and mapping skills. At the end of the primary phase children should be able to understand and apply ideas such as direction, location, scale and symbolism (Boardman, 1983). Although in the early years of primary education learning mapping skills will be rooted very firmly in the known, local environment, by the age of 11 children will have started making the transition to small-scale maps and from an atlas will be able to use the basic elements described above at continental and global scales.

If the first basic tenet of geography teaching is to work from the known to the unknown, the second is that we begin geographical education with large-scale maps and from these proceed to those of smaller scale. Large-scale maps have greater detail and cover smaller areas than small-scale maps. A 1:2,500 Ordnance Survey plan is an example of a large-scale map; an atlas map of the world is a small-scale map. It is upon large-scale maps (Table 3.1) that we focus for most of this chapter.

Table 3.1   Large-scale maps

Representative fraction	Area coverage	Space coverage
1:1250	Urban areas	500 m. sq.
1:2500	Britain but not mountain and moorland	2 km. sq.
1:10000	Whole of Britain	5 km. sq.

A number of *map elements* (Catling, 1981) exist which will

aid the teacher in the identification of what ought to be taught in primary school mapwork. These elements are:

(a) *Perspective* – maps enable us to see what is hidden at ground level.

(b) *Position and orientation* – maps show how features of various kinds are geographically related to one another and where they are located. From them directions can be given and grid systems added to aid the identification of accurate location.

(c) *Scale* – maps are scaled down representations of reality; in this sense maps are models (Board, 1967). Maps show information in different forms as the scale changes.

(d) *Map content* – maps vary in content, partly depending on scale and partly on purpose. A *street* map does not show most buildings and a 1:50,000 Ordnance Survey map uses symbols rather than shapes for many buildings.

(e) *Symbols* – because maps use symbols a *key* is required.

(f) *Additional information* – maps contain *names* of streets, buildings, woods and places. Certain maps also distinguish between different land uses (Catling and Coleman, 1981).

The discerning reader will be able to establish which of the above elements also apply to aerial photographs. While in some respects the map and aerial photographs are alike, in general maps may be said to provide more useful information. The most obvious difference between a map and an aerial photograph is that the former has names on it. Furthermore, the aerial photograph includes *everything* on the ground; the map on the other hand, includes *selective* information and does not attempt to record everything.

Developing mapping skills

A sad fact of life is that it is more common to see a map of the world on primary school classroom walls than a large map of the immediate vicinity of the school or the locality. It is true that local, large-scale Ordnance Survey plans are expensive but somehow every school should obtain one.

Local education authorities invariably have a 'blanket' licence to reproduce Ordnance Survey maps and teachers may be able to obtain such maps from teachers' centres or local libraries in order to take photocopies for school use.

Conventional thinking is that with young primary school children little formal 'map work' would be appropriate, though the large-scale plan of the local area should be displayed to reinforce the small child's sense of place. However, spontaneous mapping ('my route to school', 'my house') should not be discouraged even though the representations may be highly egocentric and iconic (Figure 1.4a). Most graphical work in the initial stages of primary education will tend to be pictorial. Imaginative picture maps can be stimulated by stories such as 'Little Red Riding Hood' and these should be encouraged. Indeed, there is every reason for the imaginative (re)construction of places found in books to continue throughout the primary school years.

Maps will come to complement pictorial representations of the environment from the age of about 7 and by the age of 9 map work should be relatively well established. It is therefore appropriate to introduce in turn the various aspects of map work which are suitable from the middle primary years.

Perspective. Initial attempts to introduce children to mapping skills might best focus on simply representing familiar objects in plan form without any scaling down being involved. Placing a pencil, an eraser or a small book on a piece of paper and simply drawing around them will familiarise children with the idea of a map representing the ground space occupied and that when observed from above it is the 'plan form' that is mapped.

The view from above can be contrasted with oblique views to reinforce the idea of the plan. An example is shown in Figure 3.1, taken from the excellent book, *Moving into Maps* (Butler *et al.*, 1984). Here children are shown a picture of a room and asked to match each object in the picture to one on a plan of the room, also provided. More simple examples include pictures of individual objects drawn in picture and plan form; more difficult relationships between picture and plan are teased out from more complex drawings and plans.

Scale. The notion of scale is implicitly introduced to children at a very early age when they play with scaled-down versions of cars, people and settlements, for example. Building bricks, dolls

This is a picture of a room.
* Colour each object with a different colour.

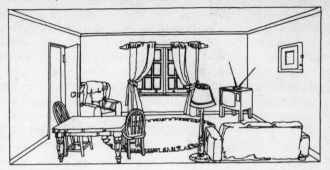

Here is a plan of the same room.

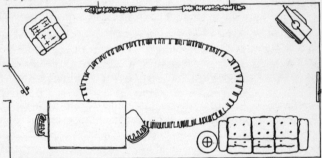

* Match each object in the picture and the plan. Do this by colouring each object in the plan with the same colour you used in the picture.

* Colour in these boxes to show the colour of the

☐ television	☐ couch	☐ rug
☐ lamp	☐ chairs	☐ floor

Figure 3.1 Converting pictures into maps forms an important skill in the early stages of the teaching of mapping skills. This example is taken from the excellent book *Moving into Maps*
(Source: Butler *et al.*, 1984)

and train sets all provide an initial experience of working with the notion of scale. We have already suggested that because boys tend to play with more 'map-like' toys than girls they are provided with an educational advantage though no hard evidence exists of a *causal* relationship.

Following the introduction to perspective, described above, children would be asked how an object bigger than a piece of paper could be represented. Initially they could concentrate on reducing an object to half size. Children would need to grasp the idea that 20 centimetres of their book will be represented by 10 centimetres on the piece of paper. The decision about what scale to use for a particular task can be introduced by children drawing a plan of the top of their desks or tables. An appropriate scale might be one-quarter or one-sixth the size though in stating the scale it would literally be incorrect to say, for example, that 1 centimetres *equalled* 4 centimetres. Rather, the scale should be presented as '1 cm to 4 cm' or '1 cm represents 4 cm.' By the age of 10 or 11 children should have progressed beyond the quarter-size reduction of desk tops, pencil cases, etc. and be able to draw a plan of the classroom. A scale of 2 cm to 1 metre might be appropriate (Boardman, 1983, 49). As well as a verbal statement of scale pupils can now be introduced to a linear scale – a graduated line from zero to, say, 6 metres. Given sufficient time it may be possible to undertake subsequent work involving the drawing of plans or maps outside the school. The playground is an obvious starting point, the scale of the map depending on the size of the site and buildings.

The *use*, rather than the construction of maps is best undertaken with small-scale (e.g. 1:2,500) Ordnance Survey maps of the locality. Measuring exercises, working out the length of streets, journey to school and to play, all reinforce the notion of scale. Measuring the distance of a curved road or meandering river may pose problems. These can be overcome – especially with older children at the junior level – by using a blank sheet of paper, marking on it distances along the road at periodic points and then comparing this to the linear scale accompanying the map (Figure 4.2). This requires great care for accurate results.

The idea of progressively smaller scales can be developed in the well-resourced school by comparing the local 1 kilometre grid square on the 1:2,500 plan with the same square on the 1:10,000, 1:25,000 and 1:50,000 maps.

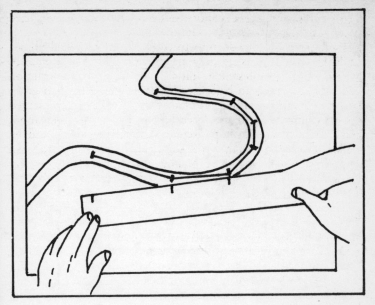

Figure 3.2   Making map measurements along a curved line using a graphic scale bar

Location. Young children can learn the relative locations of objects by recording on a flat base the places where model buildings need to be replaced if the model is reassembled the next day. Putting the models back in the right places gives children practice in recording locations and in the simple construction of a map. The learning of grid coordinates in order to specify locations more precisely than simple verbal descriptions may be related to work in mathematics or developed as part of a course on mapping skills. An initial suggestion is to conceptualise the classroom as a series of rows and columns, each row being numbered and each column being lettered. Each desk then can be individually identified by indicating the letter of the column in which it is found first and the number of the row second. Hence, the desk shaded black in Figure 3.3 is located by reference B3 (*not* 3B). A useful reminder about learning references is that the pupil goes 'in the house and up the stairs' (i.e. along the bottom row and up the column to locate the desired point). The A-Z road map could

45

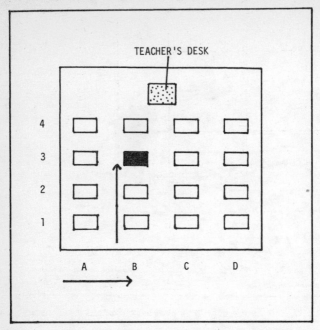

Figure 3.3   Introduction to co-ordinates by a simple map of the classroom

be the next stage in applying the idea of a simple co-ordinate system. Pupils could be asked to identify the squares in which particular parks, buildings or roads are found.

From this simple introduction we can proceed by the age of 9 or 10 to the identification of a grid square on a map by means of a four-figure grid reference. Again, a local large-scale map should be used. In this case we stress that each grid square possesses a unique number and that this can be identified by the numbers of the grid lines intersecting at the *bottom left hand corner*. In Figure 3.4 the shaded square is therefore identified as 3376.

An understanding of the four-figure grid reference can be reinforced by quizzes and tests designed to establish that children can identify features in particular squares. They can also be asked to identify squares in which prominent features are located.

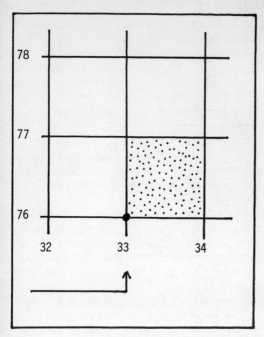

Figure 3.4 Four-figure grid references. The shaded square is identified by the reference 3376

Some pupils will undoubtedly be capable of progressing to an appreciation of six-figure grid references before the end of the primary phase. Six-figure references provide a more precise locational reference point. However, Boardman (1983, 170) feels that this skill need not be introduced until the early years of the secondary school, and many primary school teachers may therefore feel that mastering the basic mapping skills should come before ideas which can be left until the secondary phase.

Direction. Familiarity with right and left will come with growing language skills and awareness of rotation through learning to tell the time (assuming watches and clocks other than those of a digital type are used!). This would occur between the ages of 5 and 7 and map interpretation would not be attempted at this level. By the age of 8 or 9, however, pupils

47

will be ready to be introduced to the points of the compass, a basic element of virtually all maps.

The compass should be introduced by concentrating on the four cardinal points – north, east, south and west. A favourite learning aid to establish the relationship between these cardinal points is the mnemonic 'Never Eat Shredded Wheat'. The word 'WE' can also be used to remind children of the relationship between west and east.

A number of practical exercises exist to encourage children to learn direction. Pupils can be told that in Britain the sun is *south* when it is highest in the sky. The opposite direction is north and from this a line could be marked permanently on the school playground or on the ceiling of the classroom. From this children can work out the direction of 'sunrise' and 'sunset' (the sun does not actually move, hence the quotation marks) – east and west respectively. It is almost certainly unwise to introduce models of the solar system to explain day and night in the primary school and this conceptually difficult subject is best left until the ages of 12 or 13.

The four intermediate points (north-east, south-east, south-west and north-west) can be introduced following work on the cardinal points. Children might progress to the sixteen points of the compass by the final year of the primary school, but as these are rarely used except in weather forecasting they may not be a priority for many teachers.

Another practical idea in teaching direction is to place a vertical pole (jumping stand or rounders post) in the playground on a sunny morning and involve children in drawing the length of the shadow of the post in chalk every half-hour. They will observe how the shadow gets shorter towards noon and longer during the course of the afternoon. The shortest shadow will point due north and the line along this shadow is the north-south line. The east-west line will be at right angles to it and to these four directions the others can be added.

On local plans and maps children should be encouraged to work at *applying* direction to simple problems. Questions such as 'what is the name of the road at the south end of the High Street?' can be complemented with tasks involving, say, the planning of the itinerary for a local visitor, involving the use of direction to see the local sights. The application of direction can be also applied to work in a number of other spheres,

VIV RICHARDS HITS 100 !

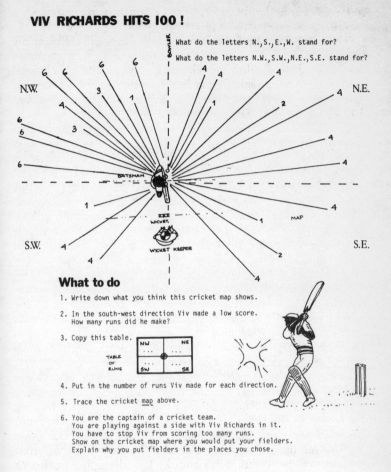

What do the letters N.,S.,E.,W. stand for?

What do the letters N.W.,S.W.,N.E.,S.E. stand for?

What to do

1. Write down what you think this cricket map shows.

2. In the south-west direction Viv made a low score.
   How many runs did he make?

3. Copy this table.

4. Put in the number of runs Viv made for each direction.

5. Trace the cricket map above.

6. You are the captain of a cricket team.
   You are playing against a side with Viv Richards in it.
   You have to stop Viv from scoring too many runs.
   Show on the cricket map where you would put your fielders.
   Explain why you put fielders in the places you chose.

Figure 3.5   Part of a worksheet used in teaching direction
(Source: McPherson *et al.*, 1985)

including weather studies (see Chapter 4) and plant growth. Records of wind direction (Chapter 4) and the directional analysis of, for example, runs made at a cricket match (Figure 3.5) further aid the understanding of an important spatial dimension of everyday life.

Symbolism. Children's early cognitive mapping reveals an absence of symbols and instead an attempt to represent the world in picture form (Figure 1.2a). The symbolic representation of various phenomena has been implicitly introduced in our discussion of scale drawings and plan forms. The desk top, the pencil case and the schoolyard are essentially represented in plan form as symbolic shapes. Such plan representation is used in the largest-scale Ordnance Survey plans but at the 1:25,000 and 1:50,000 scales map symbols come to replace the plan shapes of many buildings.

The selection of buildings and other elements of the landscape which are represented as symbols is rather arbitrary. Churches, railway and bus stations are well known; in each case a symbol, drawn out of all proportion to the ground it actually covers, represents the buildings. In other cases buildings are shown by letters (YH for youth hostel, PH for public house, for example). As well as these *points* being shown as symbols, various *patches* are likewise depicted – woodland, inland water courses, and urban areas being shaded in appropriate colours.

There seems little point in getting children to commit all the 1:50,000 Ordnance Survey map symbols to memory. If they ever use such a map they will have the symbols provided for them. However, learning the more frequently used ones (categories of road, for example) does save time in consulting the key and children certainly enjoy scouring a map for details, for its own sake.

In interpreting the best-known Ordnance Survey map, the 1:50,000 edition, one or two points of caution might be raised as this stage. Footpaths and parish boundaries should not be confused; neither should motorways and rivers, both of which are confusingly shown in blue.

In constructing their own maps children can be encouraged to develop their own symbols. However, once symbols are introduced a further important element of the map is required, namely a key to tell the reader what the symbols mean.

Relief. The height dimension is among the most difficult for young children to conceptualise in map form. However, from an early age children will have come to use vocabulary such as high-low, up-down and steep-gentle. Certainly relief elements

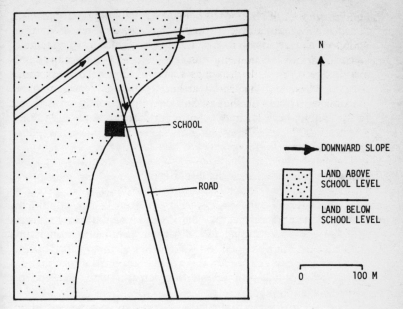

Figure 3.6   Representing relief by simple layer colouring
(Based on an idea in Schools Council, 1979)

are represented in children's picture maps (see Figure 1.2a) and
plasticine models of hills and valleys, lacking accuracy but
stressing familiarity with shapes and terminology, can be
carried out from the earliest of the primary school years.

By the age of about 8 or 9 children can be encouraged to
work on their large-scale base maps to make a simple record of
land which is either higher or lower than a well-known
landmark, e.g. the school. Selected points can be marked with a
'+' or a '−' sign depending on whether they are higher or
lower than the school itself and simple layer colouring used to
distinguish between land higher and lower than the school
(Figure 3.6). The boundary is, of course, a rough form of
contour line, but this term would not be introduced at this
stage.

The symbolic representation of relief shown on most maps is,
however, in the form of contour lines. The interpretation of
contours is not easy, Boardman (1983, 59) stressing that 'an

51

understanding of the representation of height, slope and relief on a map is probably the aspect of graphicacy which is most difficult to develop in the majority of children'. In Piagetian terms the teaching of contours is best left until pupils are moving out of the concrete operations stage into the formal operations stage. This latter stage is generally reached in the secondary school. For this reason the teaching of contour lines is probably best left out of the primary school geography curriculum.

Using mental maps of the locality

We have already seen in Chapter 1 the ways in which children represent their localities as cognitive or mental maps. It has been stressed by Catling (1978b) that such free-drawn maps possess advantages which aid the teacher in three broad areas. Such maps can be used as (a) a *diagnostic* tool, (b) an *information* guide and (c) an *instructional* activity. Each of these can be looked at in turn.

As a *diagnostic* instrument the cognitive map can be used by teachers to establish the level of the child's spatial conception and graphical representation of a familiar environment. Let us recall that on average the primary school child will be at the egocentric stage at the age of, say, 6 and at the euclidian stage at about 11. A link-picture map drawn by an 11 year old would therefore be diagnostic of limited graphical ability and the teacher could therefore take remedial action in such a case.

Children might be asked to draw and re-draw a cognitive map of their local area before and after a course on mapping skills. Comparing the two maps will help establish the extent to which learning has taken place. Cognitive maps can also be used as diagnostic tools in other contexts, for example, to establish simply how much a child has remembered or learned about a given topic.

Cognitive maps can also provide the teacher with *information* about what pupils perceive places to be like (see Bishop and Foulsham, 1973, and Spencer and Lloyd, 1974). By getting children to draw cognitive maps the teacher is able to establish which features of the landscape are important or familiar to each child. Anderson (1985) notes that if teachers take part in such mapping (drawing their own locality when they were the age of their pupils) such maps become excellent 'aids in getting students and teachers to know one another better'.

Information from children's cognitive maps can provide the teacher with ideas about which parts or aspects of the locality to explore in greater or lesser detail. Such maps also pose questions about *why* certain features and not others are so important to children. Catling (1978b, 121) suggests that an interesting corollary to this exercise is to elicit cognitive maps of children's parents and other older relatives. The differences in contents between young and older members of the community might provide useful information as parts of projects on the local environment.

As an *instructional* activity cognitive mapping might be used at the initial stage of a series of lessons on introductory mapping skills with 9–11 year olds. Children might be asked to draw a freehand map of their routes to school. Their representations could then be compared with the route as it would be shown on the local Ordnance Survey plan or local road map. Children will be alerted to the levels of accuracy and orientation by comparing their maps with the published versions. They will also become aware that different children have represented the same thing in different ways, hence necessitating the need for an agreed set of symbols. Awareness of the need for a common scale will also emerge.

Other maps

So far the impression may have been given that the only maps available for use in the primary school classroom are local large-scale Ordnance Survey plans. Although these are crucially important resources they are by no means the *only* maps with which young children should be made familiar. A wide range of maps can be introduced to children from an early age. Indeed, they invariably encounter a wide variety of maps without giving very much thought to the fact that they *are* maps.

At the lower primary stage children will have encountered maps such as those in board games such as 'Snakes and Ladders'. Such games have educational analogues and will actively aid the development of map understanding. By the middle primary stage children will have encountered a wider variety of maps, including those from newspapers, advertisements, tourist brochures and A-Z road maps. All these can be incorporated into school work, often at minimal cost to the school or teacher.

Small-scale maps

Several problems arise with the use of small-scale maps (e.g. national or international maps) at the primary school level. Although it is important that maps of the world *are* displayed and that children towards the end of the junior school years should be introduced to an atlas, the conceptual difficulties involved in the interpretation and understanding of small-scale maps should not be underestimated.

For the 8-year-old child a map of Britain is a highly abstract document. If, for example, a teacher was undertaking a project on 'Football', a dot map showing the location of the clubs of the English First Division would probably be completed quite happily by young children. However, for most of them it would be a totally meaningless exercise and the resulting map would be virtually unintelligible. Much better for the teacher to concentrate on a large-scale map of the local football stadium and its surroundings and concentrate on the impact of the club on the *local* landscape. Just as history teachers find the time dimension difficult to handle with young children, so the appreciation of distance poses great problems.

In dealing with distances at a global scale, the *time* taken for a plane to get from A to B might be more appropriate than talking in terms of distance. The fact that it takes a jumbo jet one whole day and night to get to Australia will be more meaningful to the young child than talking in terms of kilometres. The atlas might best be used to identify countries in relation to each other, to introduce children to the use of thematic maps such as political units, population or rainfall, and to become increasingly aware of the international mosaic of nations and place names. Confusion can, of course, arise when place names are written in the languages of the countries in which they are found, a tendency which is developing among some atlas publishers (Sandford, 1986). Likewise, the fact that the first atlas map that many children see is drawn according to the Mercator projection (see page 26) can cause further problems. Because each line of latitude on the Mercator projection is shown as being the same length (when, in fact, they decrease in length towards the poles), the impression is given that, for example, Texas is nearer than Alaska to Britain. Young children will obtain a perverted sense of distance and size of national units if over-exposed to the Mercator projection; a large globe is a better vehicle for an appreciation of relative national sizes and distances.

Many of the skills learned on large-scale maps and plans can be applied to the atlas in the final year of the primary school. The use of lines of longitude and latitude for global locations and the interpretation of direction at a global scale are obvious applications of ideas undertaken in local contexts lower down the school. Care should be taken in introducing relief since children frequently confuse height with slope – i.e. dark shading does not represent *steep* land.

It is also possible that atlas maps can mislead children into assuming that because only selected places are *named*, these are the only places that actually *exist*. The message relating to the use of small-scale maps is one of constant vigilance. Great care should be exercised in not assuming too much on the part of younger children in this area.

Conclusion

This chapter has ranged over a number of areas concerned with mapwork. It has been stressed that the various map elements – location, scale, direction, symbolism and relief – are best introduced on large-scale maps of the locality. We have returned to the notion of mental maps which was introduced in Chapter 1 and have suggested that these can be used in various ways in map work. And we have suggested that a wide range of other maps can be used to stimulate children's interest in graphicacy. Having stressed the use of the local area we move next to consider ways in which we can utilise the locality in other aspects of our teaching of geography.

Further reading

Simon Catling, 'Cognitive mapping exercises as a primary geographical experience', *Teaching Geography*, 3, 1978b, 120–3.
David Boardman, *Graphicacy and Geography Teaching*, Croom Helm, London, 1983.

4

Using the locality

This and the following chapter include some examples of content and teaching ideas for geography in the primary school. Of course, the potential field of geographical education is vast and the precise choice of content will depend on individual teachers, their enthusiasms and expertise. This chapter focusses on the locality as a teaching resource; the chapter which follows looks at approaches to teaching about more distant places. The organisation of this content within the overall geography curriculum is dealt with in Chapter 7.

One thing should already be clear; the locality forms a fertile ground for geographical investigation. We have so far stressed the psychological reasons for this but the local area *does* possess a wealth of teaching material at the immediate disposal of teacher and students. It is an environment to which children can immediately relate and through geographical education their awareness of their milieu can be enhanced. It is also considered desirable that at the end of the primary phase children should be acquainted with the principal features of their local area (Table 2.2).

The local environment provides children with *first-hand* insights into the world which cannot satisfactorily be simulated in the classroom. It provides a situation for field work and practical exploration and investigation. At the same time the locality provides many clues as to the interdependent nature of the world – the fact that aspects of other countries of the world are in our own homes, schools and streets. In the space of a few pages the flavour of local studies cannot be fully explored and for greater insights the reader is alerted to Mills (1981), Boardman (1983), Prosser (1982) and Palmer and Wise (1982).

Using the locality

The locality is here interpreted broadly. The child's family alone can generate a vast reservoir of geographical information on journeys, residences, locational decision-making and spatial preferences, for example. Outside the home the streets and roads contain many clues with a geographical dimension – cars, lorries, shops, houses and many other phenomena. In the locality we can make films, interview people, make plans for pieces of land, decide on locations for new residences and look at a vast range of geographical problems. In this chapter we look at some of these in the context of individual work units and their objectives.

Working with private geographies

In Chapter 1 we discussed the four traditions of geography and in Chapter 2 referred to the personal geographies of childhood. Let us return to these traditions to demonstrate briefly the way in which different approaches can be incorporated into geographical work in the primary school. In their day-to-day lives children engage in a whole range of activities which can be built on in school and related to each of the four geographical traditions. Take, for example, the building of a tree house, the construction of a bike-racing track in a wood, the cricket pitch on a waste piece of ground, or the building of an igloo in winter. For these, and many other activities in which children are regularly engaged, children can not only write descriptions but can state where and when they were built, their sizes and shapes, who was involved. Sketches and maps could be included. Pupils could attempt to answer questions based on those in Table 4.1, though it is recognised that all of these are not applicable in all cases.

Table 4.1 Questions to increase children's awareness of the geographical implications of their personal (and other) geographies

---

Spatial tradition

(1) Can the selected (   ) be mapped?
(2) What is the location of the (   )?

(3) Are activities at other locations influencing the (   )?

(4) Is the (   ) a part of a network of interconnected locations connected by pathways?

(5) What kinds of movements occur within the network of locations?

(6) Do distance and direction influence the movements between places in the network of locations?

(7) Are there any barriers preventing or influencing movements?

(8) What other factors influenced the location of (   )?

Human-environmental tradition

(1) What are the characteristics of the human-made environment where the (   ) is located?

(2) What are the best places for (   )?

(3) What are some changes that people have made in the area where the (   ) occurred?

(4) Is the environment being harmed by human activities in the area of the (   )?

(5) How have the natural features of the area influenced the activities of people living there?

(6) Are important resources for (   ) located in the area?

(7) Are people in the area trying to conserve these resources?

(8) How are human activities in the area influenced by seasonal changes?

(9) In what seasons or time of year is the (   ) done or made?

(10) How do natural hazards, such as floods, droughts, earthquakes, tornadoes, or volcanoes, affect the lives of people in the area?

Area studies tradition

(1) Is the area urban, suburban, or rural?

(2) Describe the people who live in the area.

(3) What are the economic activities occurring in the area?

(4) What is unique and distinctive about the area?

(5) How is the area similar to other areas you are familiar with?

(6) What should a good (   ) look like?

(7) What elements should a good (   ) have?

(8) What special changes must be made in the area to do (   )?

(9) Is this the only location in your region where (   ) are found or done?

Using the locality

Earth science tradition

(1) (a) What is the latitude, longitude, and altitude of the area where the ( ) is taking place?
   (b) How do each of these affect ( )?
(2) (a) What are the climatic characteristics of the area (temperature, winds, and precipitation)?
   (b) How do each of these affect ( )?
(3) (a) What are the topographical features of the area (mountains, hills, plains, and valleys)?
   (b) How do each of these affect ( )?
(4) (a) Are there water bodies in the area (lakes, ponds, swamps, rivers, oceans)?
   (b) How do each of these affect ( )?
(5) (a) What types of natural vegetation grow in the area (trees, grasses, and bushes)?
   (b) How do each of these affect ( )?
(6) (a) Do floods, droughts, earthquakes, tornadoes, or volcanoes occur in the area?
   (b) How do each of these affect ( )?

(Source: Morrill, 1985, 125)

The questions in Table 4.1 are designed to increase children's awareness of the geographical implications of their own actions, and (especially if the teacher is of a liberal philosophical persuasion – see page 32) to 'contribute to their understanding of how geographers think about places and events' (Morrill, 1985, 125). Similar geographical questions can certainly be asked about other projects at different geographical scales.

Family geographies

For every primary school child the following kinds of locational information usually exist: (a) place of birth, (b) places of former residences, (c) place of present residence, (d) place of holidays taken, (e) places where they are allowed to move locally, unaccompanied by adults, (f) places their parents were born, (g) places their grandparents were born, (h) places their parents and grandparents formerly lived. The reader may be able to extend this list. From such information a number of work units can be constructed.

Let us first consider ways in which data generated by the child's family could be used to stimulate children's interests in two broad areas: (a) the *geographical mobility* of people from place to place and the reasons for such mobility and (b) incidentally to familiarise them with the map of Great Britain and some of the places therein.

The work described here was undertaken with a class of top year (10-year-old) junior school pupils. The resources required for the introductory lesson were an overhead projector transparency of Britain and a worksheet for homework. The

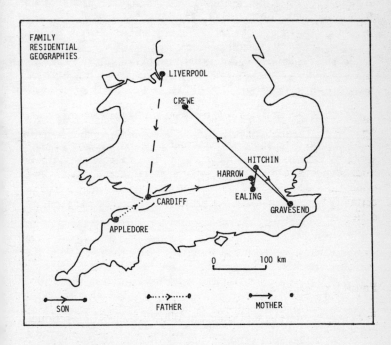

Figure 4.1   The residential historical geography of a teacher, his father and mother

teacher introduced the lesson by telling the class about his own family geography, how he had been born in Cardiff, gone to college in London, got his first job in London, his second in Hertfordshire and so on. As he talked he marked the location of each of the places named on the map and joined each one up with a line. This, he said, was part of the geography of his life. Of course, the places shown were not the only places he had been to – but they were the only places in which he had lived. He then went on to draw a similar map for his father who had been born at Appledore in Devon and who had moved to Cardiff. Likewise a map was drawn for the geography of his mother's places of residence – Liverpool and Cardiff respectively (Figure 4.1).

The teacher then posed a question to the class; *why* should such movements take place? Children were being asked to *hypothesise*, since they did not know the actual reasons for the locational decisions involved. A number of hypotheses were presented – to get a job, because their families moved, because they wanted to go to college, etc.

Next the teacher suggested that the children do the same for themselves and, for 'homework', their parents and, if possible, grandparents. He stressed that what was required was the children's parents and grandparents' places of birth and places where they had lived, in order of having lived there. In addition they had to provide, if possible, the reasons for each change of location. A worksheet (Figure 4.2) was distributed and the teacher carefully spelled out the way each child should fill it in.

For the next geography lesson the children arrived armed with the information which they had collected. The information was presented in two ways. For each child a 'family geography tree' was drawn (Figure 4.3), each tree containing the birthplaces of grandparents, parents and child. Because the children had not had much experience with the use of an atlas and because many places would have been too small to have been shown in the *Junior Atlas* which was used in the school, the teacher decided that it would be a good idea to locate birthplaces and residences by counties. Each generation's birthplaces were tabulated on the blackboard and mapped. It was found that some families had lived in the county in which the school was found for three generations. In other cases families had moved from other parts of the country and in

	PARENTS		GRANDPARENTS	
	MOTHER	FATHER	GRANDMOTHER	GRANDFATHER
PLACE OF BIRTH (and COUNTY)				
A				
B				
C				
D				
E				
F				

Why did your mother move from A to B? _____

from B to C? _____

etc.

Why did your father move from A to B? _____

from B to C? _____

etc.

Figure 4.2   Worksheet for homework on family geographies

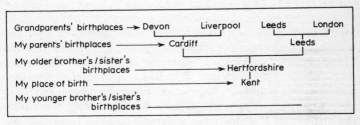

Figure 4.3   The family geography tree of a primary school child

some cases from overseas. The teacher was able to produce a list of counties with the number of birthplaces for each generation shown for each county. From this information, and with the use of their atlases, the children were able to produce a map of Britain showing geographical variations in grandparents', parents' and children's birthplaces.

This project continued with an examination of the data collected on factors influencing the decision to move. A histogram was constructed to show the differences in importance of the various factors. Questions were raised about whether mobility was greater at the present time than it had been formerly, and why.

Family historical geographies are given an added dimension if they can be traced back in time. The use of census data, for example, can be instructive and interesting. From nineteenth-century census returns a wealth of geographical, as well as historical, material can be obtained. Lead (1987) shows clearly how such data, and tithe maps, for example, can be used with children.

The geographies of present-day families have many dimensions, only a few of which can be touched on here. The location of holidays taken by families in the school can produce patterns which pose further questions. If clusters of particular locations are found to exist, hypotheses about *why* such patterns exist can be posed, bearing in mind that such work should only be undertaken by pupils at the upper end of the primary school. Through such work, a growing familiarisation with places and patterns will emerge, as a result of working with data generated by the children's own families.

The world in the home

Many teachers will wish to demonstrate to their children that the modern world is an interdependent system and that we are linked to the world through the products we find in our own homes. We return to the teaching of more distant places in the next chapter, but in any discussion of the use of the locality we should bear in mind its potential for learning about places and concepts beyond the immediate horizon.

In the fridge, freezer or cupboard, lounge, dining room or garage, there is evidence that 'the global village is not distant, but right here' (Fisher and Hicks, 1985, 39). The home and its contents are part of a worldwide network of producers and consumers. Procedures for other kinds of work in this area are found in the admirable teachers' guide, World Studies, 8–13 (Fisher and Hicks, 1985) and Figure 4.4 is used here simply to

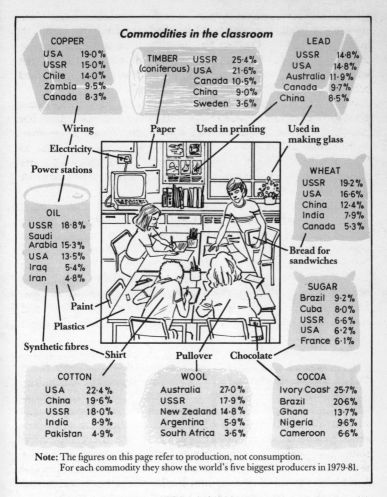

Figure 4.4   Commodities in the classroom and their global origins
(Source: Fisher and Hicks, 1985)

illustrate the potential of using the classroom, in addition to the
home, as a basis for introducing world geography.

Children can derive great pleasure from mapping the
geographical origins of other objects in the home. Polo mints

from York, the *Daily Mirror* from London, the Wedgewood ornament from Stoke-on-Trent, the Hitachi TV from Japan, the Citroen car from France, the training shoe from Taiwan ... and so on. Each letter that arrives at the house has a postmark; each telephone call has a geographic origin; the potential for mapping and graphing such phenomena is endless.

Even the language we use in the home is international. Many cultures have contributed to our daily speech. Excellent examples of the geographical use of linguistics in the primary school are found in 'Our Word House' (Fisher and Hicks, 1985, 42) and also in 'The People Grid' (Oxfam/Cockpit Arts Workshop, 1977). Examining the origins of day-to-day language can widen pupils' horizons and reduce ethnocentricity.

Places are also mentioned daily in newspaper and on television. Mapping the media is another worthwhile activity for pupils and more able children at the top end of primary schools will enjoy constructing simple cartograms (Figure 1.8) which graphically display the geographical bias present in media coverage. At the same time such maps might help generate a healthy scepticism for more conventional map projections!

Street work and field work

The locality must be explored at first hand by all primary school children. We have already noted (page 1) that insufficient attention is paid to work *outside* the school and the investigation of the local environment is strongly advocated as a prime objective of geographical education at this stage (see Tables 2.1 and 2.2). Several books (e.g. Fyson and Ward, 1973; Prosser, 1982; Palmer and Wise, 1982) have been written on the subject of local studies and in the space available we can only provide a sample of the variety of approaches which can be adopted.

When working in the locality, three broad approaches could be undertaken. Firstly, the teacher could lead his or her pupils and point out things for them to copy or write down. This exemplifies what has been termed an '*eye-balling*' approach in which the pupils adopt a relatively passive position and the work is essentially teacher centred. Secondly, the teacher could

66

introduce children to a *problem-solving* or hypothesis-testing approach which is rather more structured in the sense that the pupils know clearly the purpose of going into the local area, i.e. to solve a problem. They know what their aim is and they are not passive participants in a situation dominated by the teacher. Thirdly, we may wish to approach local work through a more *experiential* philosophy where children may make more subjective judgments about the environment, expressing their feelings and thoughts verbally or artistically. Exemplification will here be made of the second and third of these approaches.

(a) *The catchment area of the school.* In this example the problem posed was to delimit the area from which the school took its students. Staff could be included in this project if desired. The objective was to get children to work collectively in a mapping exercise which would reinforce mapping skills. Data collection was undertaken in both classroom and school yard. For each pupil in the third-year class doing the survey and for a one in ten sample of pupils in the playground, information was obtained on where they lived. Armed with this information, children were able to map the residences of each member of their class and a sample of the rest of the school's population. In an urban area residences of school pupils are usually within a mile of the school and the mapping of the school catchment could therefore be readily undertaken on a 1:10,000 Ordnance Survey map. Residences of each pupil were shown on the map as a dot and three analyses undertaken of the resulting pattern. Firstly, the number of pupils living within a 400 metre radius centred on the school was calculated; secondly the number living in each compass segment (centred on the school) was identified. The third survey focussed on each pupil's mode of transport to school. Each of these was presented in the form of a histogram. Through this approach pupils has reinforced their mapping skills, they had applied directional knowledge to a set of data, they had used simple graphics to display the results of their survey, and through map work had become more familiar with places in their local area.

(b) *Environmental appraisal.* The second example of a problem-solving approach takes the children outside the school into the streets of their local town in order to evaluate the quality of the urban landscape. This is undertaken on the 'Appraisal Scoresheet' (Figure 4.5) and is largely self-explanatory. The scoresheet as shown in Figure 4.5 could be simplified according to the age of the children with whom it was being used. Essentially it seeks to score the individual's subjective response to the landscape. Scores for a number of aspects of the urban scene range from $+5$ to -5. It involves pupils in *looking* carefully at the urban landscape. Follow-up work can seek to establish whether different individuals agreed about particular locations. Average scores for each location could be calculated and the results mapped. Teachers might be able to adapt the scoresheet for use in rural areas and undertake simple forms of landscape evaluation.

(c) *Town trails*. 'The essence of the town trail', wrote Fyson and Ward (1973, 43), 'is sensory experience'. Basically trails seek to develop perceptual awareness which all too often seems to lie dormant in our day-to-day lives. Town (they could be village or rural) trails are planned in that an itinerary is identified on a map to include particular points of interest, interspersed with relatively less significant stretches. At least one high viewpoint should be included. At each stopping point pupils can:

- study the 'floorscape' (i.e. nature of pavings, road materials, etc.);
- identify the character of the street furniture;
- look for plaques on walls;
- ascertain dates of buildings;
- collect patterns on bricks and stones (including rubbings);
- evaluate different ways of building houses and shops;
- listen to street noises;
- breathe in the air and note variety of smells;
- say if they like or dislike the particular spot and why.

Children can, of course, develop their own trails. They can design itineraries for potential visitors to their locality, highlighting interesting places on a large-scale map and annotating these with key items of information. Pupils might also produce 'anti-trails' – routes which contrast with 'official' sightseeing tours. A wide range of trails could be drafted by teachers and/or pupils; industrial trails, recreational trails and

Environmental appraisal sheet No. .... Name .... Location of viewing area Date										
Description of area										
Scores	+5	+4	+3	+2	+1	0	-1	-2	-3	-4	-5
1. Visual aspects (a) appearance (b) condition (c) relationships to surroundings (d) scale of buildings (e) trees and shrubs (f) street furniture (g) tidiness (h) surprises											

2. Traffic
 (a) Moving
   (i) noise
   (ii) danger
   (iii) smell
   (iv) ugly
 (b) Parked
   (i) danger
   (ii) space available
   (iii) delivery access											

3. People popularity
   Do people seem to
   enjoy the area?
   Can they walk freely?											

Tracker's likes and dislikes Total + −											

Figure 4.5   Environmental appraisal sheet
(Source: Fyson and Ward, 1973)

history trails are the most obvious complements to the more well-known nature trail.

(d) *Feelings about the environment.* Teachers with a more humanistic disposition will wish to use the locality as a source for expressive work in writing or art. Essentially, this approach attempts to get children to articulate their feelings about place, landscape or environment with minimal input from the teacher. The purposes of such work can be numerous. For example, expressive work such as that being described here can be neither 'right' or 'wrong', being the child's response to the environment. It is therefore the child's own personal record – something in which the child can take a personal pride. Let us describe an actual example of such work.

A teacher was interested in developing in her class a personal response to the environment, in this case a secluded woodland in the middle of the countryside. She wished to *use* the environment as a milieu for creative writing and as a medium for developing sensory awareness. In addition, she was anxious for the children to develop an attitude towards the environment which would lead to a respect for the countryside. The class were taken into the wood and asked to sit down at least 2 metres from their nearest neighbour. They were asked to close their eyes and keep absolutely quiet for five minutes and try to clear their minds. They were to simply listen to and 'feel' the woodland.

After five minutes they were asked to articulate their feelings. Some said it was restful, others that it was quiet; some children said the woodland was peaceful and that they welcomed the absence of cars and noise. The children then formed themselves in pairs and one member of each pair was blindfolded and the partner asked to place his or her partner's hand against a piece of vegetation. The blindfolded person spent a minute or two literally feeling aspects of the woodland and then proceeded to another piece of vegetation. This was repeated about five times. The blindfold was then taken off and an attempt was made to identify the things that had been touched and handled.

The teacher then asked the children to think about the value of the woodland and asked what they would feel if it was threatened with removal for the development of a housing estate.

On returning to school the class were asked to compose a poem about their experience in the woodland. Some sensitive and caring pieces of work were produced.

Planning scenarios

Related closely to field work are a number of approaches which grow out of local issues or events which require a planning solution. In every locality there will be such a problem. The local press will carry articles about such things as the location of the new bypass, the new motorway, the gypsy site, a new supermarket, a new sports centre and so on. There is every reason for pupils to be involved in their own enquiries into these kinds of local problems. In such cases they become involved in what Kohn (1982) called 'real problem solving', i.e. the problem is not an academic problem, as in role play (see page 128), but a *real world* problem which will actually affect children's lives.

One simple example can illustrate this idea. In this case the teacher wanted to develop in his class an understanding of two important ideas. The first was that land use change involved *planning*; secondly, that land use change might involve a *conflict* of interest within the community and that different people might view the change in land use in different ways.

Pupils in a village primary school were aware that a piece of land behind the village hall (Figure 4.6) had been given to the village for use as a recreation area. The first thing the teacher did was to take the class of 9-year-olds to see the site so that they were fully familiar with it. They absorbed its dimensions, looked at the trees, saw how close it was to the main road and other residences and generally familiarised themselves with the site. The teacher introduced the planning implications by asking them what their parents would have to do if they decided to extend the size of their house. The popular response was that they would have to consult 'the council' and from this the teacher informed them that it would be the Planning Department of the council who would be involved. The class were encouraged to discuss *why* planning permission was needed for changes in land use. Notions of conservation and pollution were mentioned.

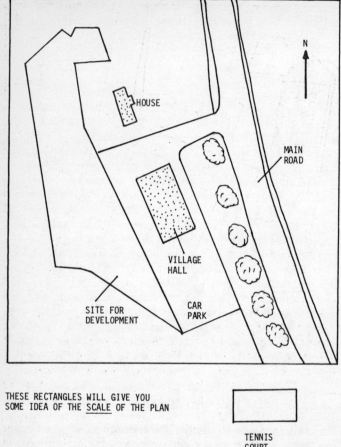

THESE RECTANGLES WILL GIVE YOU
SOME IDEA OF THE <u>SCALE</u> OF THE PLAN

TENNIS
COURT

SMALL
BOWLING
GREEN

Figure 4.6   Base map for planning scenario

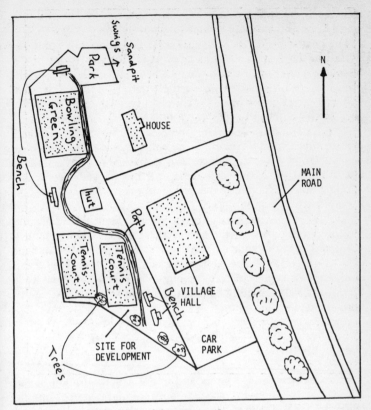

Figure 4.7   A child's plan of the proposed recreation area

The class then met to discuss the application for the change in land use. A class discussion was held, pupils working in groups and discussing possible problems which might result from the development of the land for recreational use. The teacher was available to answer any queries and circulated around the groups as they worked. After about half an hour's discussion, spokespersons for each group gave the groups' decisions about what should happen to the land.

The teacher told the class that in this case planning permission *had* been obtained to change the land use from farmland to recreational usage. A proviso in the planning documents was that no play could take place behind the residence next to the village hall (see Figure 4.6). The children readily appreciated why this should be the case.

The next step was for the children to decide how the land use should be developed. What form of recreation provision should be made, assuming that funds could be made available? Should provision be for children or for the elderly? Or for both? The children first undertook a school survey during playtime, eliciting from fellow pupils the kinds of things potential users of the site might want. This information was collected and transformed into a histogram. The children were next provided with a large-scale outline of the site and asked to plan it, taking into account what they had seen and heard. They were also asked to write a 'planning report' on a prepared form, provided by the teacher (Figure 4.8).

The teacher alerted the chairman of the committee responsible for the development of the site to the children's work. It was suggested that the children's work be displayed at the annual general meeting of the committee and this was done. The children had been involved in planning their own land use; their ideas were carefully considered and in some cases actually implemented.

Data collecting

On the doorstep, in the street and in the neighbourhood of the school can be found a vast amount of data which can be collected and analysed to explore geographical ideas and situations. Consider first of all the school grounds. One of a series of excellent ideas about teaching about the local environment and undertaken in a Birmingham primary school (Palmer and Wise, 1982) was an examination of the nature of environmental problems in the schoolyard. The pupils concentrated their attention on litter and initially divided it into certain categories. For one week litter was collected, sorted (into the categories – paper, glass, polythene, metal/wire, etc.), counted and weighed. Over 12,000 pieces of litter were collected in one week! A number of mathematical exercises were undertaken on this impressive collection of data. Pie charts and histograms were constructed and the average amount of litter per square metre calculated. Palmer and Wise

BETLEY SPORTSGROUND PROJECT

SURVEYOR'S REPORT

NAME OF SURVEYOR: Emma Shannon

DATE OF SURVEY: 23rd November 1983

LOCATION OF LAND TO BE SURVEYED: The field behind Betley Village Hall Cheshire.

DESCRIPTION OF LAND AT PRESENT: A sloping piece of land with seven trees. It slopes to south east.

PROPOSED FUTURE DEVELOPMENT: Make it into a Activity Park. With tennis court, crazy golf and jogging course. with trees and benches.

EFFECT ON LOCAL RESIDENTS: Some more cars than before. Some more noise too

ANY OTHER COMMENTS: Noisey play should not be allowed near houses.

Figure 4.8 Planning report of the proposed recreation area

(1982) describe other such environmental work in their excellent book *The Good, the Bad and the Ugly*.

In the street outside the school equally impressive sets of data are easily collected without leaving the 'confines' of the school premises. One teacher was interested in having his class undertake a project on 'Transport'. He wanted the children to learn that a substantial proportion of the cars on our roads were not British but were imported from France, Japan and Germany. He knew that several members of his class knew a large amount about cars and could easily recognise the makes as they passed by the school. Those with limited knowledge of such things were engaged in collecting the total number of different types of transport passing the school during a 20-minute period. Buses, lorries, cars and bicycles were carefully recorded, each child being responsible for a different type of vehicle and each direction of movement accounted for. The 'car experts' had the job of identifying the makes of each car which passed the school on each side of the road.

After 20 minutes the class returned to the classroom and began to collate the data. The total number of vehicle types was tabulated; the names of the cars were identified and assigned to the country in which they were made. The children then presented the information in the form of a histogram and the number of cars from each country located on a world map, ready prepared by the teacher. The children had to find Japan, Germany, France and Britain and decide how to depict the information they had collected. Some chose proportionally drawn bars; others attempted to draw little cars, proportional in number to those observed outside. Finally, the teacher asked the children to invent a title for each of their pieces of work.

Once the school buildings are left behind and children move into the locality it is essential that certain precautions are taken to ensure safety. The permission of the head teacher will be required – and in some cases that of the LEA too. Letters to parents should also be written, informing them of what is happening, specifying type of footwear required if necessary, and reminding them that the outdoor work in geography *is* actually going on in the school!

It may be necessary to obtain some help from adults other than teachers for such outings. Parents, friends, local sixth formers, students from the local college education department can all be approached. In order to minimise danger (and teacher stress) children should always work in twos and threes and should not be spread over an unreasonably large area. They should work within well-defined limits, e.g. two lamp posts, two trees, or specified buildings. Usually such an outing need not take much longer than one hour. Notebooks, clipboards, prepared worksheets and maps need to be distributed. The presence of cameras can often lead to an enhanced experience.

Many places in the locality could be visited and Scoffham (1980) provides several good examples of the kinds of local environments in which primary school pupils can engage in fascinating studies. We can illustrate this type of work by describing the potential for geographical study in the church-yard or graveyard, assuming one is sufficiently close to the school. Often such visits will assume an inter-disciplinary flavour, perhaps being part of a project or topic, but explicitly geographical work which could come out of a graveyard visit include (a) the examination of directional aspects of the erosion of gravestones, (b) the calculation of rates of erosion, (c) the identification of the residences of those buried in the graveyard, (d) the subsequent mapping of such information (to produce what an American geographer once sacrilegiously described as a 'God-shed') and compose poetry or creative writing about the 'feel' of the graveyard environment. Allied to these approaches they could take rubbings from gravestones, seek evidence of infant mortality, calculate the average life expectancy for different time periods and collect devotional poems (Scoffham, 1980, 70).

Data could likewise be collected for many other locations near and around the school.

Weather and climate

So far we have been concerned almost entirely with human aspects of the locality. There are, of course, a large number of physical-geographic aspects of the environment which can be illustrated and explored locally. Like other aspects of geography, the weather and its effects will have been experienced at first hand before children start at primary school. These experiences can be used to provide a basis on which to describe weather and climate encountered in more remote environments. In addition it should be remembered that the importance of weather to human beings should always be given emphasis (Table 4.2).

Table 4.2   The way in which weather conditions affect people's daily lives should be given emphasis

---

Weather also affects anyone who is travelling. Think about this. Then copy out the table and fill it in to show how different ways of travel are affected by each kind of weather.

Weather condition	Car	Train	Aeroplane	Ship
High temperature				
Frost				
Snow				
Ice				
Rain				
Fog				
Strong wind				

For all aspects of weather local observations and recordings do not require expensive equipment (Figure 4.9). Indeed, young primary school children can experience differences in temperature by simply standing in the sun and in the shade; they can describe the differences in the wind in sheltered and exposed locations. The effect of weather conditions on clothing styles can be discussed; children can wash old clothes and establish which environments (in sun, wind or shade) the conditions for quickest drying are found. These simple ideas provide the basis for more detailed and scientific work in a number of different aspects of local weather observation, each of which can be described in turn.

(a) *Wind*. As with other forms of weather, children can relate the daily effects of the wind to different groups of people who welcome or dislike windy days. They can develop records of wind direction with the help of a simple weather vane and record direction on a wind rose. Simple classificatory systems (simplified versions of the Beaufort Scale) can be developed (Figure 4.10).

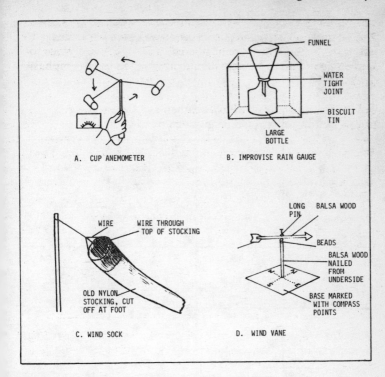

Figure 4.9   Improvised equipment for weather recording
(Source: Firth, 1981)

The effects of wind can be readily simulated in the classroom by the use of a hairdryer applied to sand and other objects. In addition, national patterns of wind direction can be established by monitoring weather maps of the television news and in the daily newspapers. It should be remembered, however, that wind direction is described by the direction of its origin rather than its destination (i.e. westerlies come from, NOT go to, the west).

(b) *Temperature.* At the lower end of the primary school, temperature might be recorded by simply recording whether it is hot or cold on a 'weather board'. More graduated terms like

Using the locality

IN EACH SPACE DRAW PICTURES OF WHAT HAPPENS AT DIFFERENT WIND SPEEDS (SOME HAVE BEEN DRAWN FOR YOU). WHAT MIGHT HAPPEN AT WINDS SPEEDS 4 AND 9?

Figure 4.10 Relating wind speed to readily observable phenomena. Numbers refer to the Beaufort Scale

warm, chilly or mild can be introduced later. Again, we can look at the impact of temperature by considering those who like (e.g. ice cream salespersons) and dislike (e.g. office workers) say, hot weather. The effects of weather on local environments can be stressed. For example, cold weather can lead to the freezing of roads, while hot weather can contribute to forest fires.

Using a simple thermometer children can take daily weather records and may be able to identify local differentiation in temperature. For example, the school itself might be explored as a kind of 'heat island'.

(c) *Rainfall*. All primary schools should have a rain gauge, and while lower stage primary school children may record rainfall on a simple dichotomous scale (i.e. wet/dry), rainfall measurements should be able to be taken quite accurately by the top end of the primary school. The quantity of rainfall is not the only thing that may be recorded. Local variation in rainfall can be established if two or more rain gauges can be located in the immediate locality of the school; the duration and intensity of rainfall and its relation to wind direction can be examined. Precipitation in the form of snow can be measured for depth in different locations and the characteristics identified of local places where snow remains the longest. Local rainfall records can be compared with those of other places. By the end of the primary phase children should be aware of the hydrological cycle and this can be illustrated by simply taking two dishes with the same amount of water in them, placing one indoors and one in the schoolyard, and seeing what happens. Other suggestions for dealing with the hydrological cycle at the primary school level are provided by Oaks (1974).

Local rock types

Within the locality a range of rock types will exist, either in their natural geological settings, or as building stones for houses, churches, walls, etc. Children will be familiar with local quarries and other rock exposures and full advantages should be taken of visits to such sites. Samples of rock can be collected and tested for various characteristics. At a basic level this might mean simply distinguishing the rock on the basis of hardness, colour, coarseness, etc. More sophisticated tests can involve a large number of criteria, however. An example of a detailed recording sheet is shown as Figure 4.11.

The uses to which different rocks are put can be examined in the local area by looking at roads, houses, and other buildings. It may be possible to chart the geographic origins of the different rocks being used.

The *formation* of rocks may be considered in the upper part of the primary school, not simply by children being told of the three main types and their presence or absence in the local area, but through the experimentation in the classroom with sand and water, for example, to illustrate the formation of sedimentary rocks. Samples of sand of different particles can be shaken in water-filled bottles to demonstrate the formation of strata in sedimentary rocks.

The physical landscape

The local landscape will invariably possess features of physical as well as human interest and primary school children should be encouraged to explore local landscapes with a view to understanding their nature and origins. Lakes, hillsides, valleys and coastlines all have stories to tell and the first-hand acquaintance with these landscapes should be starting points for enquiry.

Some excellent suggestions for work on streams have been made by Bowles (1981). For children of about 7 years of age it is suggested that the most simple stream studies are simply the identification of the direction along which water runs in local gutters – i.e. downhill. From simple observations it may be possible to infer the location of former parent streams (Figure 4.12). The idea of a network is implicitly introduced. As children reach the upper stage of the primary school more sophisticated techniques can be gently introduced. Many home-made aids can be constructed – tapes from knotted string, plumb lines from heavy screws on twine, floats from corks or even orange peel, ranging poles from bamboo canes graduated in 10 cm lengths and levels from a protractor with plumbline (Bowles, 1981, 42). Stream velocities can be measured at different points on the long and cross profiles. Many other

RECORD SHEET FOR ROCK TESTING   Date :

Name :		✓ or X in these boxes where possible					
Name or number of rock sample ...							
1. Have you cleaned it and dried it out ?							
2. How many different materials does your sample seem to be made of ?	1						
	2						
	3						
	More						
3. Does it sparkle and shine like glass ?							
4. Does it feel ?	. . . rough ?						
	. . . smooth ?						
	. . . gritty ?						
	. . . soft ?						
	. . . hard ?						
	. . . sticky ?						
	. . . crumbly ?						
	. . . sharp ?						
	. . . powdery ?						
	. . . tacky ?						
	. . . silky ?						
	. . . flaky ?						
5. What happens when you put a drop of acid on the rock ?	it fizzes strongly						
	it fizzes weakly						
	it does not fizz						
6. Try to scratch the rock	Will your fingernail scratch it ?						
Rub the scratch with a wet finger to clean it	Will a knife blade scratch it ?						
7. How many grams ...	... does it weigh when dry ?						
	... does it weigh after soaking 3 minutes?						
	... of water did it soak up in 3 minutes ?						
8. Where was it found ?							

Figure 4.11   Example of a recording sheet for local rock survey
(Source: ILEA, 1981)

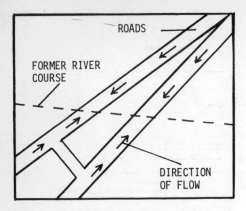

Figure 4.12   Street slopes, direction of flow
of water and past river courses

suggestions for similar work in the context of coastlines and
soil sections can be found in Bowles (1981).

Practising mapping

The local area can obviously be used for reinforcing the wide
range of mapping skills discussed in Chapter 4. Reading and
using maps is best achieved in the local area and all work in the
locality should incorporate reinforcement and practice of map
skills already introduced and taught in class. Following routes,
recognising where we are 'on the map' and filling in blank
spaces on the map (Figure 4.13) are all skills which can be
practised within walking distance of the school. Even a short
walk in some areas can take in a variety of landscapes, both
human and physical, and a carefully prepared worksheet can
aid the further development of the exploratory instincts.

Knowledge of the locality

It has been suggested that by the age of 11 children should be
able to identify conspicuous landscape features of their locality,

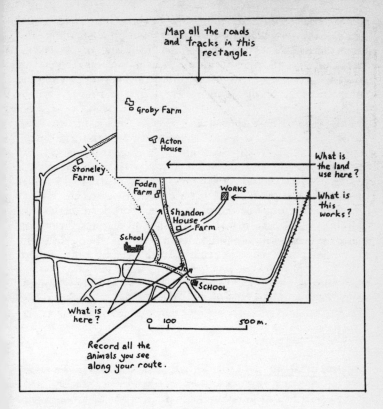

Figure 4.13   Base map for map work exercise in the locality

have some understanding of the nature of the settlement in which they live and of the ways in which the surrounding land is used, be aware of changes which are taking place and have some appreciation of the ways in which the activities of people, especially themselves and their families, are influenced by the character of the place in which they live and its location (Bennetts, 1985, 307). Such general guidance is helpful but begs a number of questions. Key phrases are 'be aware of' and 'some appreciation of'. It is not clear, from such terms, whether pupils should simply *know* or should also be provided with

85

some germs of *understanding*. Children can readily learn the name of the rock type under their feet, but understanding how it got there is conceptually more difficult. Likewise, it is easy to learn that unemployment is at a high level in certain towns, but why the local economy is in such dire straits may be beyond the comprehension of the teacher, let alone the primary school child.

This chapter has stressed the *use* of the locality to learn particular skills and general concepts. But it seems reasonable that in so doing a large amount of factual information will inevitably, and often incidentally, spill over into the child's consciousness. Studying local map sheets will provide local place-name information. Tests on direction will teach children where one place is in relation to another. Work in the locality will highlight local relief and geological features; work on planning issues will alert students to where planning decisions are made. It is increasingly recognised that the learning of place names for their own sake is a waste of time (see page 1) and that much of the former 'capes and bays' type of geographical work, be it at the local or international scale, is best left to the last five minutes of lessons when quizzes on such subjects can be undertaken.

Sensitive issues?

It has been suggested that many textbook authors are incapable of recognising a controversial subject when they see one. In most localities controversial or sensitive issues abound. However, as Storm (1970) put it, many teachers find it easier or more convenient to ignore such issues and instead distribute a set of class texts on some totally remote topic. It can be argued that sensitive issues should *not* be ignored at the primary level. Indeed, the Schools Council curriculum project *Time, Place and Society, 8–13* (Derricott *et al.*, 1977), in using a number of sensitive themes with young children, discovered that the children had 'grown in confidence and competence in handling these issues' (p. 15).

Sensitive issues which may involve teachers presenting perspectives to children with which their parents may disagree should be dealt with carefully. Teachers themselves need to evaluate their own attitudes. If, for example, a survey of leisure provision highlighted the fact that certain areas of a city were not provided for adequately, should the children accept this (with an air of 'informed inactivity') or should they engage in some form of direct action? As Derricott *et al.* (1977, 15) note, the 'propensity for analysis to indicate the need for social action can put the unprepared teacher into an embarrassing situation'. In Chapter 7 we consider some suggestions for appropriate behaviours which might be generated by the inculcation of particular attitudes in the classroom. However, at this stage we should stress that the extent to which teachers encourage children to engage in social action (e.g. writing to the local press, trying to get their parents to stop buying fruit from particular countries, etc.) is one which should be undertaken with full consultation with the headteacher. It is not unknown for teachers to contact parents by letter, especially if their co-operation is sought in obtaining their views on local issues of a controversial or sensitive nature.

Field work and school journeys

Given the relative flexibility of the primary school timetable, work outside the school buildings should pose few organisational problems. An extension of field work is the residential field trip in which children will be away from school for several days and this involves a greater degree of planning and organisation. Many local authorities have their own residential field studies centres which provide wardens and instruction. In other cases the teachers are responsible for developing field teaching and the appropriate worksheets and resources. Whatever the situation, such residential field visits require very careful planning and supervision. Tragic events indicating negligence by teachers serve to illustrate the responsibility teachers have for children in such situations. Places for field visits should be selected carefully, to meet the requirements of the journey's educational objectives. Planning for a school journey should start as much as a year in advance of the dates of the journey. Many local authorities provide guidance about planning such visits and a useful timetable to illustrate the stages involved is shown in Figure 4.14.

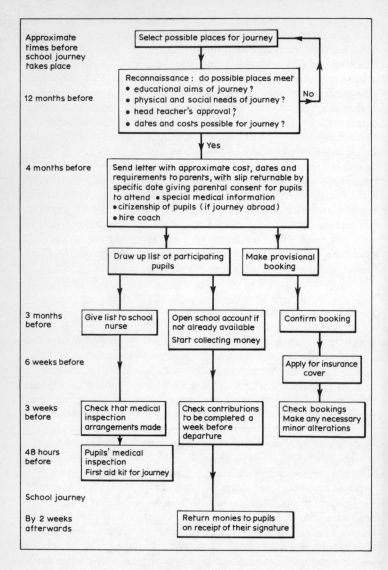

Figure 4.14   Administrative arrangements for a school journey
(Based on ILEA, 1981, 30)

Conclusion

The locality provides a highly fertile source of ideas for teaching geographical skills, ideas and facts. It not only acts as a source for local exemplifications of a variety of geographical phenomena but also provides an entry point to world studies and it is to a more explicit concern with more distant places that we turn in the next chapter.

Further reading

David Mills (ed.), *Geographical Work in Primary and Middle Schools*, The Geographical Association, Sheffield, 1981.
ILEA, *The Study of Place in the Primary School*, ILEA, London, 1981.

5

Far away places

We have stressed so far that much work in the primary school should be grounded in the locality, using large-scale maps to which children can most readily relate. However, throughout the primary years children will be aware of more geographically distant images (the nature of which were discussed in Chapter 2) and, especially towards the end of the primary phase, there is a strong case for including some content from more distant places. Apart from satisfying children's natural curiosity about their world, an understanding of the modern world demands at least an introduction to some aspects of foreign countries before children enter the secondary school. Cognitive and affective aims are advanced by studying other places. Teachers are also likely to feel that some media generated images of foreign places need to be countered.

Bennetts (1985, 307) has stressed that:

> the study of unfamiliar places deserves greater attention than it is often given. Pupils should begin to explore similarities and differences between their home area and more distant places. One of the challenges for teachers preparing such work is to provide pupils with information and experience that is rich enough to capture their imagination and to enable them to appreciate conditions which are different from those with which they are familiar.

Of course, for many primary school children more distant and unfamiliar places do not simply refer to those in foreign countries. As Barker (1974, 116) reminded us, 'to very many children in Liverpool, Lancaster is as different and distant as Marseilles' and a heterogeneous group of young children is likely to contain members of very varied geographical experiences and horizons. Some will have visited America on holiday; others the Isle of Wight and others will not be able to afford holidays involving travel over any significant distance from their homes.

This chapter addresses a number of problems associated with the teaching of more geographically distant places. For example, *which* places should be selected for study, accepting that global coverage is impossible? What questions ought children to be asking about distant places? How can we avoid stereotyping and racialist overtones? What kinds of maps should be used in teaching about foreign places? How do we begin to explore with younger children the processes which have produced regional differentiation? We try to answer some of these questions in this chapter. We commence with a brief consideration of factual coverage.

Which facts should they learn?

Even at the primary level parents often wring their hands in despair at the apparent lack of 'geographical literacy' on the part of 10- and 11-year-old pupils. Their concern is essentially about the seemingly limited amount of *factual* information children appear to have about the world, capitals of different countries being apparently unknown and the names of longest rivers being incapable of instant recall. But what facts about the world *should* children know when they leave primary school?

An article in the *Geography Teacher* in 1918 suggested that at the age of 16 students should have learnt 500 place names, 200 of them in the British Isles (Orford, 1918, 214). Few teachers would be as dogmatic as this today, but a nagging worry remains about what degree of factual knowledge should be retained by our children. Are some facts more important than others? Is there a threshold size below which it is unreasonable for pupils to know a city's national location? Should a child of 10 be able to name all the continents? And to be able to locate them on a map of the world?

Cole and King (1968, 15) suggested that 'a sensible criterion for what should be memorized and what looked up when needed seems to depend on the amount of time required to do one or the other.' If we constantly need certain factual information it is worth learning it; if we need it only very infrequently it may be better to know a *source* of information from which it may be found. It might also be worth knowing how to use the source of the information (i.e. a map, atlas or encyclopedia).

Facts which are constantly bombarding our senses tend to be those which are close to home (see Chapter 1). It *is* useful to know the countries which are close to Britain (if you are British) and it is useful to know something about the physical geography of various parts of Europe. But it is also *interesting* to know something about other places in the world too.

As Storm (1970) pointed out, many children may be 'much more interested in volcanoes, Australian aborigines, coral islands than in plotting the distribution of lamp posts or making a map of the cycle sheds'. Our educational philosophies need not be entirely utilitarian and the pleasure of learning for its own sake should never be extinguished.

Manson and Vuicich (1977, 191) state that 'intelligent informed citizens know where important places are located'. Such a simple statement begs a number of important questions. For example, does location refer to absolute (i.e. as defined by a coordinate system) or a relative (i.e. in kilometres, or perhaps better, hours, or indeed cost) location? In answer to these kinds of questions it seems reasonable that by the end of the primary phase children might be expected to know that Cardiff is a coastal city in South Wales; it seems unreasonable that they should know it is at 51° 30 north of the equator and 3° 13 west of Greenwich.

Selecting places to study and questions to ask

The choice of places to study will depend on a number of factors. Working from the immediate and the known has already been suggested in our discussion of the way in which world geography can be stimulated by materials in the home and classroom (page 64). At the lower end of the primary school stories based on folk-tales set in unfamiliar locales and books by foreign authors about their own countries will increase children's range of geographical awareness. Topic work on 'animals' or 'plants' will likewise increase children's knowledge of global contrasts.

As we progress through the primary school, we may begin to base our choice of places on those visited by members of the class, places in the news, the personal experience of the teacher, the availability of suitable stimulus material in the cupboard, the popularity of a television soap opera (learning about *Dallas*, for example), sports events like the Olympic Games or World Cup; all these are good stimuli for selecting particular places.

Other teachers may feel that they have a duty to specify particular places which, for example, increase children's knowledge of the north–south divide, the east–west division or conflict in Latin America, the Middle East or Northern Ireland. Whatever reasons are used for selecting particular places it is important that a reasonable spread of geographical locations is selected. An introduction to *world* geography (albeit selective coverage) does not mean *European* coverage or *African* coverage. Selected places from a number of regions is more desirable, providing children with a good basis for comparing and contrasting life in more distant places with that at home.

An earlier discussion focussed on the use of large-scale maps and it is important to reiterate that in studying more distant places it is again best to look at relatively small areas in some depth. Obviously, there is a need to set the place in some global context, but once study has begun a relatively small area will be most appropriate for children of primary school age.

Having identified a place to study in which our objectives can be achieved, the kind of questions we might ask about a place (Bennetts, 1985, 307) might include:

Where is this place?
What does the place look like? What are the main features of the landscape?
Do many or few people live there and why?
What is it like to live there?
In what ways are people's activities and ways of life influenced by the character of the place and its location?
How have people made use of or modified the environment?
Do many people visit the place and for what purposes?
What important links does it have with other places?

In what ways is this place similar to, or different from, our
home area?
What are the reasons for the main similarities and
differences?
Is the place changing in character and, if so, why?
What do we feel about the place? What do we find attractive
or unattractive about it?
Do we think that the changes taking place are an
improvement or not?
What are the views of the people who live there?

These questions are by no means exhaustive nor are they
sequential. They may not all apply to all subjects or all places.
However, they are the kinds of questions geographers ask
about places and they do provide useful guidelines for course or
lesson planning.

An example of the application of some of these questions to
a particular place can be illustrated by part of a work unit on
Florida, in the USA. As the teacher had visited Disneyworld,
she felt that this would be a motivational way of interesting
children in certain aspects of the modern American landscape.
She was especially keen for her pupils to learn that (a) Florida
was in the USA, (b) it was warmer than Britain, (c) Disneyworld
differed in scale from typical British holiday resorts, and (d)
Disneyworld differed from other parts of Florida (e.g. the
Everglades). In terms of skills, she hoped to provide her pupils
with practice in map work and in applying their map work
skills to the planning of a hypothetical theme-park on the
Disney model in their own country and highlighting the
advantages and disadvantages of such developments.

The teacher's initial motivational stimulus was to probe
children's mental maps of Florida. Where was it? What did the
children know about it? Was it warm or cold? Varying answers
were provided, including television programmes (*Miami Vice*),
information about the Kennedy Space Centre and oranges.
These and other images were written on the blackboard to
remind children of their initial perception of the place they
were going to study. The teacher then selected 7 or 8 slides of
Disneyworld in order to catch the flavour of the place which
the class was going to look at in more detail. The images which
were intended to be communicated by the slides were crowds of

holidaymakers, warm weather and the kind of provisions found at Disneyworld. Having established where Florida was in the USA and where Disneyworld was in Florida (near the city of Orlando) the teacher presented the class with a worksheet containing a map and questions to be answered. Included on the worksheet was a *semantic differential* profile (Figure 5.1) – a series of bi-polar adjectives from which children could construct their personal and class profiles of their feelings towards the place they were studying.

Problems of stereotyping and bias

'Bias – stereotyping – racism' constitute a spectrum of attitudes and behaviour which we have already discussed in our coverage of children's mental maps (Chapter 2). It is unlikely that bias can be totally eliminated, though it can be significantly reduced. We have suggested that stereotyping presents inaccurate images of peoples and places and should therefore be countered by the presentation of more accurate images. A 'hunters of the frozen north' approach is stereotypical because it generalises rather than specifies; it labels the north and it labels the people as hunters. By taking a small part of 'the north' and looking in depth at one group of people and the way they live, such stereotyping could be reduced.

Racism poses a greater problem, given the word's varying interpretations, but there can be no denial of the seriousness

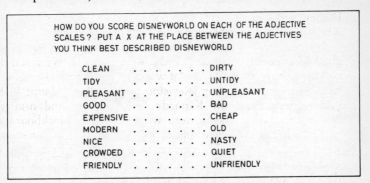

HOW DO YOU SCORE DISNEYWORLD ON EACH OF THE ADJECTIVE SCALES? PUT A X AT THE PLACE BETWEEN THE ADJECTIVES YOU THINK BEST DESCRIBED DISNEYWORLD

CLEAN	. . . .	DIRTY
TIDY	. . . .	UNTIDY
PLEASANT	. . . .	UNPLEASANT
GOOD	. . . .	BAD
EXPENSIVE	. . . .	CHEAP
MODERN	. . . .	OLD
NICE	. . . .	NASTY
CROWDED	. . . .	QUIET
FRIENDLY	. . . .	UNFRIENDLY

Figure 5.1   A semantic differential list

with which even the most 'establishment' bodies view the problem of 'the pressing issue of racism in schools and in geography teaching' (Walford, 1985, 20). The Geographical Association, for example, has committed itself to an explicitly *anti-racist* (*not*, let it be noted, non-racist) policy, urging teachers to condemn and counter racism (Table 5.1). Here we have an example of geography teachers being encouraged to teach attitudes and moral values (Maye, 1984, 33).

Table 5.1   The Geographical Association's Statement on Anti-Racism.

The Council of the Geographical Association affirms its intention:

1   to encourage all geography teachers
    a)   to consider what forms of behaviour might justifiably be regarded as racist
    b)   to develop their own and their pupils' awareness of racism – both in the textbooks and materials they use, and in their own and their pupils' contribution to lessons
    c)   to condemn such racism
    d)   to consider how geographical education may best seek to counter racism;

2   to support geography teachers in efforts to create greater awareness and concern amongst their colleagues about racism, and to develop overt anti-racist policies in their schools;

3   to examine the Geographical Association, its committees, its Branches, its publications and activities, for racism and racist practices, and to act against these;

4   to encourage all GA Branch Committees to develop their own and their members' awareness of racism and to support anti-racist courses for local teachers.

(Source: Walford, 1985, 21)

A practical suggestion for detecting bias is provided by Fisher and Hicks (1985, 107–8) who suggest that in enabling pupils 'to identify with the humanity of others and to challenge negative stereotypes' we require both materials which contain positive and negative images of particular countries and peoples. The best materials to use are probably those produced by the group which is stereotyped. For example, in teaching introductory work on aspects of the indigenous peoples of North America, quotations from indigenous groups are useful. Several excellent examples are found in books produced by the Institute of Race Relations (1982a, 1982b) which while generally pitched above the level of the primary school child provide numerous illustrations and quotations for use by the teacher. An example is shown in Table 5.2.

Table 5.2   Native Americans may view historical geography differently from us

---

"You tell all white men, 'America First'. We are the only ones, truly, that are 100 per cent. We therefore ask you while you are teaching school children about America first, teach them the truth about the first Americans.

We do not know if school histories are pro-British, but we do know that they are unjust to the life of our people – the American Indian. They call all white victories, battles, and all Indian victories, massacres.

History books teach that Indians were murderers – is it murder to fight in self-defence? Indians killed white men because white men took their lands, ruined their hunting grounds, burned their forests, destroyed their buffalo. White men penned our people in reservations, then took away the reservations. White men who rise to protect their property are called patriots – Indians who do the same are called murderers.

White men call Indians treacherous – but no mention is made of broken treaties on the part of the white man . . .

White men call Indians thieves – and yet we lived in frail skin lodges and needed no locks or iron bars. White men call Indians savages. What is civilisation? Its marks are a noble religion and philosophy, original arts, stirring music, rich story and legend. We had these . . ."

Grand Council of American Indians, 1927

(Source: Institute of Race Relations 1982a)

Ideally, the teacher should provide pupils with resources which highlight the positive attributes and the skills and values of indigenous lifestyles. Common feelings can be stressed, emphasis being placed on similarities to, rather than differences from, ourselves.

The next step is to alert children to the injustices such people suffered in the past, stressing particularly how it felt from their point of view. The example in Table 5.2 is instructive in this respect. Having alerted children to the injustices suffered by such peoples, the class can be encouraged to look at the ways in which various groups are presented as stereotyped. What do words like 'primitive', 'savages', 'backward', 'Indians' (as in USA) really mean? What other words could we substitute more accurately for these?

Minority groups: exotic or exploited?

In teaching about distant places the teacher will invariably wish to draw on children's curiosity about peoples who have traditionally been presented as exotic or bizarre. However, motives for teaching about minority groups can go beyond the tapping of children's interests in 'far away places with strange sounding names'.

Minority groups and the treatment they have received at the hands of majorities certainly provide an important source for teaching about racism and exploitation. Fisher and Hicks (1985, 102) have provided a useful checklist for teaching about minorities and this is shown in Table 5.3.

Let us consider an actual work unit on aboriginal Australians which was designed to counter stereotypical thinking, taking account of the items in the checklist in Table 5.3. Initially, the teacher dealt with historical-geographic background to aboriginal life, showing the class pictures of their settlements and describing their self-sufficient and egalitarian lifestyle prior to the invasion of Australia by Europeans. The illustrative materials were taken from *Patterns of Racism* (Institute of Race Relations, 1982a). The teacher then provided a case study of one present-day aboriginal settlement in Queensland, based on the worksheet shown in Figure 5.2. It should be noted that a large-scale map was adopted and the exercise exemplified both cognitive and affective learning, i.e. the learning of facts about how aboriginal Australians presently and formerly lived and the exemplification of mapping skills, plus the opportunity of developing empathy with the minority group being studied.

Where possible work on foreign countries should be

Table 5.3   Teaching about minorities: a checklist

---

1. *Motives*
What are your reasons for choosing to teach about a particular
minority group? Is it merely because they appear colourful or quaint?

2. *The present*
Will the study look at the present situation of the particular minority
as well as its past and at the issues which confront its members today?

3. *Status*
Will the study show the social and economic status of the minority
group and its disadvantaged position in society as regards the
majority?

4. *Prejudice*
Will the study acknowledge the presence of prejudice and
discrimination in majority/minority situations?

5. *Origins*
Will the study consider the origins of the minority situation, e.g.
colonisation, migration, separatism?

6. *Empathy*
Will the study attempt to foster sensitivity and empathy for the
minority experience? Will it attempt to combat prejudice in any way?

7. *Culture*
Will the study look at the minority group's culture and history in a
positive way, including views of minority group members themselves?

8. *Victims*
Will the study make it clear that the minority group itself is *not* the
problem, or will it blame the victims for their own oppression?

9. *Response*
Will the study show the breadth of minority response to
discrimination, ranging from despair to direct action?

10. *Self-esteem*
What would be the likely effect of this study on the self-image and self-
esteem of children from that, or other, minority groups?

(Source: Fisher and Hicks, 1985, 102)

grounded in the lives of real people undertaking typical
routines. If possible their lives should be contrasted and
compared with those of children's own families. In recent years
school television programmes (see page 122) have increasingly
provided excellent materials of this kind and such detailed and

Far away places

Look at this map of an aboriginal settlement in Queensland, Australia. The lines with numbers on them are called contour lines. They tell you how high the land is above sea level.

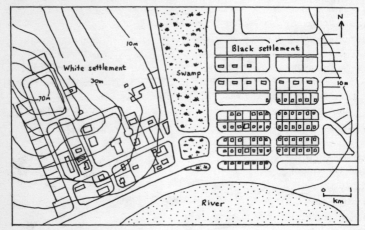

Put these labels in the correct column of a table with two headings, "Black Settlement" and "White Settlement".

unpleasant · crowded · most likely to flood · pleasant · higher ground · healthy · lower ground · low population density · high population density · grid planning · open planning

What aborigines say about their land:

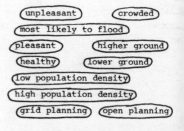

> **"** Comalco never asked for this land . . . part of this land is mine. It is our forefather's land. We cannot give it away . . . No we don't want the money. We don't want the company to take our land . . . I still stand up. I am fighting for my land. **"**
>
> *Albert Chevalthen, an Aboriginal elder, 1978*

Now try these questions:

1. Do you think the aborigines will get their land back? Give reasons.

2. If they had their own land how might their lives be different?

3. If the land belonged to the aborigines why did the company take it away?

Figure 5.2   A worksheet on modern-day aboriginal settlements

realistic materials provide the pupils with superior insights to those dependent solely on the medium of print.

However, realistic materials can stimulate thought and learning if presented in the form of, say, a diary written by a person from another part of the world. Supported by large-scale sketch maps and photographs of the environment in which such people live, a good learning resource can be developed. Part of such a resource is shown in Figure 5.3 and describes a day in the life of a 30-year-old Ghanaian woman. Accompanying worksheets (Connolly, 1986) involve the children in constructing a pie-chart of the daily time-use (divided between sleeping, walking, working in the home, farmwork, and other activities). Children are also asked to think about ways in which Mabla's tiredness could be reduced, whether her working day is longer than her husband's and how villagers might best use a loan from Oxfam. Readers may be able to think of a number of other exercises based on the considerable amount of information shown in Figure 5.3.

Physical contrasts

Most children in the British primary school will never have experienced the climate of the tropical rain forest, the icy conditions of Antarctica or the hot desert of north Africa. Neither will they have been likely to have experienced the visual splendour of the Rockies or of the Great Barrier Reef. It is almost impossible to simulate such conditions in the classroom and for this reason problems arise in deciding how best to communicate such impressions to children.

It is again best to root any discussion of distant climates in what the children have experienced in their own, day-to-day, lives. A rare heat-wave in Britain would represent a common-place temperature in certain parts of the world; parts of Wales receive twice as much rain as many parts of England; it is darkness for almost six months at the North Pole. Through an appreciation of what, say, 20°C. *feels* like pupils will gain an initial awareness of what a 'hot' or 'very hot' place is like.

From an awareness of what temperature figures are used to describe 'hot' climates children can utilise their daily newspapers to discover which parts of the world experience different

Far away places

MABLA'S DAY

Mabla is a 30-year-old woman who lives in Bolgatanga, Northern Ghana. She is responsible, like most of the other women in the village, for growing enough food for the family's needs. She also sells some food to get cash. She is married and has 4 children; a girl of 12, 2 boys of 10 and 6 and a baby girl of 2. Children are important to parents in Ghana and they plan their families carefully. Mabla's family lives in a village compound.

TIME	ACTIVITY
4.00	I get up, feed the baby, tidy up and light the fire for cooking breakfast — if only we had electricity like they do in the cities in the south! Sometimes my 12-year-old daughter helps me too.
5.00	I wake up my husband and two sons. Next I give the family breakfast, feed the chickens and then I eat last of all.
6.00	I set off for the fields. It's a 3km walk and takes about half an hour, so I like to get started before the sun gets too hot. We have special farming jobs, the men do the clearing of the land (although we help them sometimes) and the ploughing and the women do the planting, weeding, protecting the crops from pests and harvesting, all using traditional tools. We also process the crops which means we turn them into something we can eat. It's the women's job to store them too, so that the food lasts until the next harvest.
11.00	I walk 2km back towards the direction of the village to collect the firewood I need for cooking, and take it another 1km back home where I leave the wood, pick up food for lunch and take it back to the fields with some water from the well which is ½ km away from my house. If I had electricity in my village life would be easier! A tap near the house would help too!
12.00	We have lunch in the fields. All the village women work nearby and we help each other out. You have to work when you're pregnant, but you rest for three weeks after the baby is born. We take our babies and young children to the fields with us.
13.00	I work again for another 3 hours. We often sing to make the time go quicker.
16.00	Farmwork is over for the day, although there's still plenty to do. We all go back to our village and the women pick up firewood on the way. I don't need to collect water as I can send my daughter because she'll be back home now. All children between the ages of five and twelve go to the school which the villagers helped to build two winters ago in the dry season. I'm very proud of my children doing so well as it might mean they have an easier life than me. It does make farm work more difficult though, as they can only help in the evenings and at weekends and holidays. I also have to pay for their books.
16.30	My daughter fetches the water. She helps me by looking after the baby while I pound 'foo-foo' — it's like a dough made out of water and vegetables. You have to hit it hard for a long time, then you make into dumplings and cook it with soup. I wish they'd invent an easier way of doing it, it's hard work. I have to remember to feed the chickens too.
18.00	I'm still doing the dinner while my husband goes to the village meeting on making improvements in the way we farm. They say if we use machines and chemicals we'll be able to grow more food. The men are clubbing together to buy a tractor for ploughing. I hope they think about how to make the women's work easier after they've sorted that out. It would mean more work for us if they ploughed up a bigger area of land, more work using our old fashioned tools.
19.00	I serve the family meal and we all eat.
20.00	I clear away the meal, tidy up, wash up and finally have a bit of time to do some sewing. It's getting dark, so we have oil lights — I think about electricity again!
21.00	I go to bed now because it's an early start again tomorrow. It'a such a hard life I often think about the city; I've heard that things are easier there.

Figure 5.3   Mabla's day
(Source: Connolly, 1986)

102

kinds of temperatures on the previous day. It is not only the world of political and economic facts which the newspapers provide us with, and the daily report of weather conditions round the world forms an excellent resource for the teaching of world climatic regions. Indeed, if local weather conditions have been recorded they can be compared daily with those in say, New York, Brisbane or Aberdeen. The only way to actually *experience* foreign weather conditions in Britain is to do so in artificial conditions. Access to a garden centre or a botanical garden in which tropical plants are cultivated can give children a real feel for conditions in the rain forest. Likewise, the effects of very cold climates on the disintegration of rocks can be simulated with the help of a freezer and a saturated piece of chalk.

Vegetational and land-form variations from place to place are best introduced through visual aids such as slides and pictures. Many excellent photographs of distant environments are found in such sources as the *Geographical Magazine*, the *National Geographic* and the Sunday colour supplements. Such readily available materials can be used to construct useful wallcharts.

Common concerns

The impression given so far may be that the emphasis in teaching about distant places should be on *differences* between people in such locations and ourselves. However, it is obvious that all peoples have similarities as well as differences in the sense that all people require food and shelter and all cultures produce artistic forms of various kinds. Children who in English or Art are 'encouraged to create their own poetry, painting, dance, literature or handicrafts can readily understand and appreciate the art of other countries' (Seefeldt, 1977, 158). Art, handicrafts and food from other countries can be sampled and examined. Different housing styles around the world can be compared and contrasted, as can clothing and footwear. We have already stressed geographical aspects of language (see page 66). All of these approaches stress common needs, though they are expressed differently.

Stressing common aspects of humanity is important in the

primary school because in the early years of formal education it seems that children tend to focus on differences between peoples rather than on similarities (note page 25). Teaching children that similarities also exist may help reduce their distrust, fear and stereotyping of other peoples and places.

Conclusion

Three basic points have been stressed in our consideration of teaching about distant places. First, we need to be aware of dangers of stereotyping and racism though it is accepted that bias in coverage will be difficult to avoid. Indeed, it may be desirable to bias coverage of areas in which the teacher has greatest expertise, interest or first-hand experience. Secondly, it has been stressed that where possible coverage of distant places should be undertaken with large-scale maps and should relate to real people and their daily lives. The third point to stress is that at all times coverage of distant places should be related back to the locality and the child's own experiences, not simply to enable the child to identify more easily with the topic under consideration but also to stress the interdependence of the modern world.

Many ideas which can be used in teaching both about the locality and about more distant places were discussed in Chapter 5 in our examination of the use of the locality. We also include such ideas in the chapter which follows, in which we consider different classroom strategies for geography.

Further reading

Simon Fisher and David Hicks (eds), *World Studies 8–13: a Teachers' Handbook*, Oliver & Boyd, Edinburgh, 1985.

Nance Lui Fyson (ed.), *The Development Puzzle*, Hodder & Stoughton/CWDE, Sevenoaks, 1984.

6

Classroom styles

This chapter tries to identify different classroom strategies which contribute to effective learning in geographical education. In a sense we attempt here to provide some guidance for those who want to be 'good geography teachers'. However, the criteria by which we evaluate and assess 'good teachers' are far from clear. A successful pedagogue who fills children's minds with the wrong sort of geographical knowledge may, in one sense be a good teacher. On the other hand, a teacher whose knowledge of geography is encyclopedic but cannot convey it to his or her students may be a good geographer but would fall at the first hurdle in the race towards satisfying some teacher evaluators. It is hardly surprising therefore, that some observers believe that 'too much emphasis is given to teaching' (Ball, 1972, 7) and that more ought to be placed on learning. In other words, ought we to be creating environments for learning rather than courses of content for teaching?

This question has been posed rhetorically but at least part of the present chapter focusses on learning situations in geography. Before considering some of the situations and classroom strategies which we might employ at the primary school level, it will be germane to consider the way pupils themselves view teachers and what, in their eyes, constitutes a 'good teacher'. Table 6.1 identifies 29 statements which together might go to make up many children's 'good teacher', if we could answer 'often' to every one of the statements. How many of us would want our children taught by someone for whom the answer was 'never' to each of the statements?

A well-known tenet of teaching is that the classroom strategies should be varied. This chapter concentrates on the

Table 6.1   A checklist of teacher qualities. Do your children answer 'often', 'sometimes' or 'never' to each of these?

---

1   My teacher enjoys teaching.
2   My teacher keeps me interested in my school work.
3   My teacher knows what to do and how we are going to do it.
4   My teacher is friendly.
5   My teacher cares about my feelings.
6   My teacher is patient and understands me.
7   My teacher lets me know if I am behaving right or wrong.
8   My teacher is polite and courteous.
9   My teacher does things to keep us well-behaved.
10   My teacher is fair when students misbehave.
11   My teacher teaches in ways that help me learn.
12   My teacher uses things like charts, filmstrips, films, records, overhead transparencies, videos and the computer.
13   My teacher chooses things such as texts, equipment, supplies, and worksheets that help me learn.
14   My teacher gives clear directions and explanations about my class work.
15   My teacher explains things again if I don't understand.
16   My teacher listens to me and uses my ideas.
17   My teacher tells me when my answers are right or wrong.
18   My teacher talks and writes so that I can understand.
19   My teacher teaches things in an order that makes sense.
20   My teacher uses more than one way to teach.
21   My teacher works with large groups, small groups, and individual students.
22   My teacher gets me interested in new lessons.
23   My teacher gives me a chance to do things in class.
24   I work or pay attention during a whole lesson.
25   My teacher does things to keep me working or paying attention during a lesson.
26   My teacher tells me why the things we learn in school are important.
27   My teacher knows a lot about what is taught in school.
28   My teacher uses the whole class period for teaching and learning activities.
29   My teacher makes my classroom look like a nice place to be.

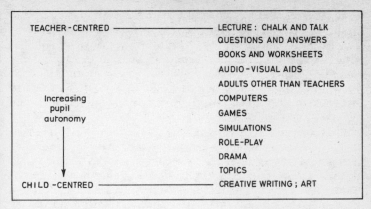

Figure 6.1 A spectrum for teaching and learning strategies for geographical work in the primary school

variety of approaches the teacher can make in classroom and out of doors.

Broadly speaking we can conceive of the variety of teaching approaches as stretching from the teacher-centred to the pupil-centred end of a spectrum (Figure 6.1). At the one end will be the didactic, 'chalk-and-talk' style of approach; at the other will be the kind of work characterised by projects, discovery learning and drama. In what follows we attempt to illustrate different kinds of classroom approaches, taking in both ends of the spectrum and a number of positions in between.

Talking to children

A considerable amount of time is spent by teachers in talking to children. Three particular aspects of teachers talking are appropriate to the geography classroom. Firstly teachers need to be aware of the length of time they take talking to children; secondly teachers need to be aware of the nature of the questions they put to children; and thirdly there is a need to constantly be on guard concerning the nature of the vocabulary used in geography teaching.

It may be possible for primary school children to sit entranced for half an hour listening to a good story about

107

distant places. But this time-span of concentration is untypical. Many undergraduate students will be aware of a lapse in concentration and attention in lectures after, say, 25 minutes. Obviously, the precise time will vary depending on the topic and the teacher, but lapses in attention do invariably occur. How much more difficult it must be for a child of 7, 9 or 11 to concentrate on a not particularly interesting subject for more than a few minutes. It is therefore surprising to find that one study revealed that primary school children spent 57.7 per cent of the school day listening 'despite studies that indicate people are poor listeners' (quoted in Stephenson, 1984, 16). Many primary school children will start fidgeting after five minutes of monologue – understandably, of course. There is therefore the need to break up monologue and replace it with dialogue.

When question and answer sessions take place in geographical studies there is a need to consider the nature of the questions, as well as the answers. For example, some questions are simply factual, either asking for names (e.g. Teacher: what is that instrument called? Pupil: a thermometer) or information (e.g. T: What is it used for? P: for measuring temperature). Other questions may involve reasoning, either based on calculations (e.g. how many metres in 5,000 centimetres?) with the aid of factual recall or on reasoning without recall (e.g. T: Why do you think the public house is located at grid reference 473567? P: Because that grid reference marks a point near the centre of the village which would make the pub within easiest reach of local residents).

In all these kinds of questions it is quite possible for pupils to provide wrong answers. Such wrong answers should not be followed by negative comments from the teacher, nor denigration which reduces the self-confidence of the child. A caring teacher will encourage, not discourage, children giving incorrect answers. Williams (1981, 13) argues that particular attention needs to be given to the 'pseudo-open' question, i.e. one for which there appears to be many answers but for which, in fact, the teacher only wants one specific response. For example, if we have the question 'Why are reservoirs found in valleys in mid-Wales?' at least three correct answers could be given, i.e. (a) to provide water for English cities, (b) because of the suitability of the valleys for dam construction, or (c) because of the heavy rainfall in that part of Britain. The teacher *could* have asked for as many different answers as possible but often the teacher wants one answer. With such pseudo-open questions there is always the danger that a correct response is brushed aside.

We might also want to guard against an overemphasis on purely factual questioning, since the tendency is often for pupils to engage in inspired (or uninspired) guesswork. Instead, concentration on questions which involve reasoning, thinking or understanding might be a better use of time.

A third important area involving teachers talking relates explicitly to what is sometimes (misleadingly) called 'geographical vocabulary' (misleading because according to at least one geographical approach, *anything* can be 'geographical' if it can be subjected to geographical study – see page 4). The problem often arises, however, when words used commonly in geography lessons have quite different connotations in everyday life. 'Relief', 'basin', 'mouth' and many other such homonyms are matched by an almost equally large number of homophones (e.g. beach–beech) or near homophones (e.g. desert–dessert). Such vocabulary can cause considerable confusion to young children who have not yet been initiated into the geographer's way of using certain sounding words. Research by Milburn (1972) stresses that it is especially 'important to ensure that geographical terms which are common to everyday speech are presented in their geographical context'.

The problems of interpretation can be illustrated by some of Milburn's research findings. Of 47 'geographical' terms given to first-year junior school children, less than 9 per cent of the definitions provided could be broadly described as 'correct'. By the fourth year the percentage of correct definitions had risen, but only to around 30 per cent (Table 6.2).

Table 6.2 Familiarity with 'geographical' vocabulary

Junior school year	Number of terms in test	% 'correctly' defined
1	47	8.8
2	81	12.2
3	165	14.6
4	215	29.7

(Source: Milburn, 1972, 114)

The implication of these kinds of findings is that in primary (and secondary) school, apparently simple terms may be used by the teacher on the assumption that no explanation is required. Great care should be taken to ensure that words are used in the correct context and that children clearly understand the meanings applied to them.

So far we have considered teachers talking and said very little about children saying anything themselves. While pupils' questions are often encouraged, they are equally often answered directly by the teacher without allowing the pupil to 'think aloud'. A particularly common question is the simple 'Please Sir/Miss (sic), what's the title?' The teacher need not answer this question but instead suggest that the children think up appropriate titles for themselves. Likewise when a pupil asks questions like 'Where is Texas?' the teacher might most usefully respond by asking the child to *think* about how he or she might go about finding out where Texas is.

When pupils give incorrect or inaccurate answers to teachers' questions, such wrong answers should be built on rather than dismissed. As Williams (1981, 19) puts it, 'we must *never* discourage pupils from answering questions when they have been asked'.

As a general rule questions from the teacher which are thrown open to the class (e.g. 'Has anybody got any questions about what we've done on rivers?') elicit responses from fairly predictable members of the class (i.e. extroverts and/or boys). If a pupil's name is specified, more members of the class can be involved. Teachers may have to make a conscious effort to involve boys and girls equally in classroom discussion, even at the primary level.

Children might be encouraged to talk more often than they do in geographical work. We return to ways of organising pupils' talking in our section on role play and simulation, towards the end of this chapter.

Using books in geography

Recent decades have witnessed a revolution in geography textbook publishing which has transformed the somewhat dull monochrome text to a bright and visually attractive learning resource. For the first time there is something of an embarrassment of good geographical material for use in primary education. Three broad types of commercially produced books exist and we can briefly exemplify each type. Individual titles referred to here are intended to be illustrative and reflect the author's particular biases. Teachers wishing to purchase class sets should always obtain inspection copies following perusal of publishers' catalogues and decide for themselves which books fit their own situations.

The first group of books which could be reasonably used as class sets contain a number of titles whose specific objective is to aid the learning of mapping and other spatial skills. A truly innovative series, *New Ways in Geography* (Cole and Beynon, 1969, 1982), includes three primary level texts and one lower secondary book. A more recent book in this category is the colourful *Outset Geography* series (Catling *et al.*, 1981) which provides a well-structured course for the primary years and includes a very wide variety of highly imaginative teaching ideas. Also in this group one might include a multi-authored book originating from Australia called *Moving into Maps* (Butler *et al.*, 1984). Each of these books build on sound psychological principles and upon research into children's mapping abilities.

A second type of book which is less likely to be purchased by teachers as class sets but instead in smaller numbers is that which seeks to guide children in their enquiries into the local area. In many cases teachers may feel that one copy of such books is sufficient for them to adapt material to their own situations. Examples of such books include the 'Finding out About' series intended for upper primary and lower secondary pupils. One example, *Finding out about Villages* (Charlton and Bentley, 1983) provides good guidance for various kinds of village studies. Another series called *Looking Around* (Lines, 1984) adopts a systematic approach, dealing with topics such as power, industry and natural disasters. *Going Places* (Renwick and Pick, 1979) attempts to provide a course covering the four years of the junior school and commences with introductory mapping skills and proceeds to work related to more distant environments.

A final group of books are those which attempt to introduce young children to more distant places, latter-day equivalents of

'Children of Other Lands'. An interesting attempt to explore the world's variety of lifestyles is found in the *Storyline Geography* series (published by Oliver & Boyd) which combines fact with fiction to introduce children to global contrasts and varying physical environments.

In addition to these three types of books, it should be noted that at the top end of the primary school pupils will each require access to a good primary atlas.

In evaluating textbooks a number of considerations might be taken into account. Wright (1985) identifies ten possible questions to ask of any text being considered for class use. These are:

1 Is an apparently cheap book durable enough for my needs or is its true cost only discovered when it falls to pieces after two weeks?

2 Is the book written at the appropriate language level? Reading ease can be established by applying various indexes, the Flesch index being among the most well known. This involves taking 10 random samples of passages of 100 words and ascertaining the number of syllables per 100 words (wl) and the average number of words per sentence (sl). Reading ease is then established by calculating $206.835 - 0.846(wl) - 1.051(sl)$. For primary school children the scores should always be more than about 80 (Graves, 1979, 166).

3 Is the book up to date, both factually and methodologically? In some books the impression is sometimes given that places such as South Wales are still dominated by coal-mining or that the impact of oil in desert areas of the Middle East has yet to occur.

4 Is the book interesting or does it fail to identify topics to which modern children can readily relate?

5 Does the book contain a range of different kinds of exercises (see Chapter 7).

6 Is the book in full colour?

7 Is the book's design cheerful and interesting?

8 Are maps and diagrams easily comprehended or are they cluttered?

9 Does the book suit *me* and *my* pupils? Because of the many books which are currently available it is important for teachers to be fully aware of the variations which exist within the range.

10 Is the value-system of the book acceptable? Does the book provide both sides of an argument? It is worth, for example, checking the sources of photographs (Wright, 1985) since many

Table 6.3   Towards sex equity in primary school geography

Sex equity analysis

Directions

1. Using your textbook, list these items:
   - number of pictures of men or boys;
   - number of pictures of girls and women.

2. Using the pages of your book, list the page numbers for the following:
   - 10 pictures of men or boys doing something active (e.g. talking rather than listening);
   - 10 pictures of women or girls doing something active (e.g. playing football rather than watching).

3. List the kinds of places in which men and women are found in pictures in your textbook.

---

may originate from national embassies and multi-national corporations and hence give a somewhat perverted picture of reality. It is also important to check for racist, sexist and ageist material in text and illustrations. Pupils themselves can analyse books for such -isms (see Table 6.3).

In addition to the commercially produced textbooks from the well-known publishing houses, there is the need to be aware of a vast amount of published material emerging from a large number of other sources which can be used by teachers in geographical work. Various industries, trade unions, local authorities, government sources, and travel agents, for example, may provide free but useful material for teaching. In addition, national and local newspapers and magazines provide a wealth of geographical material which the teacher can use in the construction of resource sheets (see below) or stimulus material.

Resource sheets

Despite the variety of textbooks which exist, many teachers may prefer to tailor their own resources to their classes' needs. In the production of a worksheet 'there is much to be learnt by looking critically at professionally produced materials' (Martin, 1986, 97) such as textbooks, newspapers, comics or travel brochures. Maps, cartoons, pieces of text or advertisements appearing in these kinds of media can be adopted or adapted as part of a worksheet and complemented by the teacher's supporting questions and comments. The advantage of utilising newspaper material is its topicality – something school texts cannot hope to match. Children can also readily identify with local newspaper materials.

Excellent guidelines for producing resource sheets are provided by Martin (1986) and Gerber (1985). The following points should be borne in mind:

1   Keep the text in a compact block and not written from side to side of the sheet.
2   Keep the text in sequence so the reader does not have to move around the sheet unnecessarily.
3   Use typewritten, rather than handwritten text, if possible.
4   Include stimulating, provocative and humorous illustrative visual materials if possible.
5   Use bold headings and instructions.

An example of a worksheet designed for 10- or 11-year-old primary school pupils is shown in Figure 6.2.

Using photographs

Visual materials, either from textbooks or provided individually by the teacher, are good sources for developing a number of learning skills. These include careful observation, acquiring information from a visual source, analysing and evaluating information, empathising with different peoples in the situations shown, and producing a written interpretation of a visual image (DEC, 1985, 8).

A number of suggestions for using photographs in the classroom have been provided by material produced by the Development Education Centre in Birmingham (DEC, 1985, 68–73). One example will be provided here in order to illustrate the potential in the use of photographs in geography.

An excellent idea for encouraging enquiry in children is to present them with a 'question grid' similar to that shown in

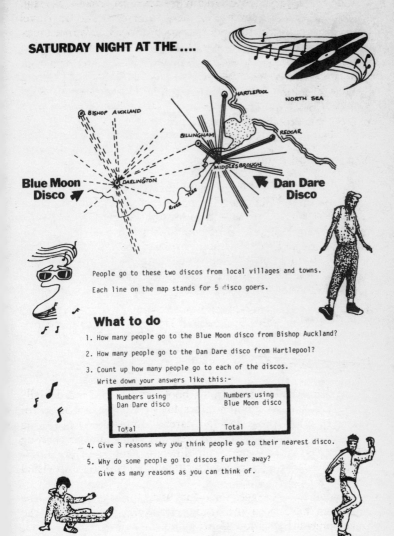

SATURDAY NIGHT AT THE ....

People go to these two discos from local villages and towns.

Each line on the map stands for 5 disco goers.

What to do

1. How many people go to the Blue Moon disco from Bishop Auckland?

2. How many people go to the Dan Dare disco from Hartlepool?

3. Count up how many people go to each of the discos.
   Write down your answers like this:-

Numbers using Dan Dare disco	Numbers using Blue Moon disco
Total	Total

4. Give 3 reasons why you think people go to their nearest disco.

5. Why do some people go to discos further away?
   Give as many reasons as you can think of.

Figure 6.2   Worksheet for top primary school pupils
(Source: McPherson, 1985)

Classroom styles

Figure 6.3. Children initially work on these questions and photographs individually and then discuss their individual responses in groups of four. Discussion usually ensues about different interpretations of the photographs and the different things people in the photographs may have been talking about. Having answered the questions, the pupils are then asked to (a) provide a caption for the photograph and (b) to work in pairs and develop a question grid of their own based on another photograph provided by the teacher.

Cartoons and comics

Cartoons can be used in geographical work, since they provide both topical and humorous stimuli for pupils' work. Provocative cartoons can provide a basis for debates, a focus for research and the injection of humour. In addition children can be encouraged to create their own cartoons or complete an unfinished comic strip. Almost all daily newspapers contain cartoons suitable for incorporation into worksheets or for use as overhead transparencies. One publication possessing great potential for geographical work, the *New Internationalist*, has many cartoons and comic strips which could form the basis of work on a very wide variety of topics. An example is shown in Figure 6.4.

Adults other than teachers

The catchment area of the school will contain a large number of people who are potentially useful in assisting the teacher in work of a geographical nature. These include not only parents or relatives who may be of assistance on field trips, working in a supervisory capacity, but also those who can actually make a useful contribution to learning by relating their own experiences. Such people are not only those in possession of 'traveller's tales' about distant places but also local parents who can possess many insights denied to the teacher.

Bassey's (1978) research found that the most common adult visitors to classrooms (apart from teachers) were the police and the clergy. Only 8 per cent of respondent teachers cited parents as being involved as classroom visitors. Yet parents of a

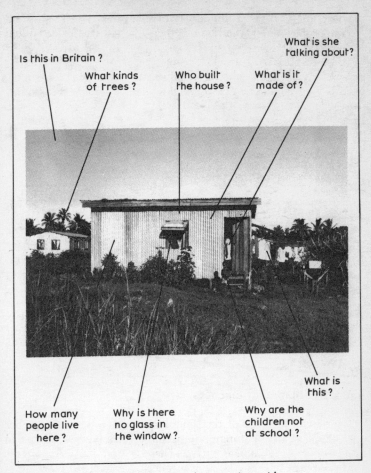

Is this in Britain?

What kinds of trees?

Who built the house?

What is it made of?

What is she talking about?

How many people live here?

Why is there no glass in the window?

Why are the children not at school?

What is this?

Figure 6.3   Example of a photographic question grid

school's population will possess a vast reservoir of information about a range of geographical topics. Some parents may be planners, others builders, others lorry drivers and farmers. Used carefully, such experts can enhance greatly work undertaken on a variety of topics. Interviewed by children or left to present material themselves, such adults can often provide much-needed variety in the primary school classroom.

117

Classroom styles

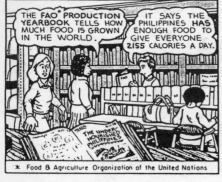

* Food & Agriculture Organization of the United Nations

118

Figure 6.4 Part of a comic published as part of the *New Internationalist*, July 1983. Cartoons and comics provide useful stimulus materials and can be complemented by an appropriate worksheet or set of comprehension questions

119

Audio and visual aids

Geography, more than many other fields of knowledge, lends itself to the classroom use of a wide variety of audio and visual aids. The large number of possibilities in the use of film, video, audio tapes, records and slides, as well as the, nowadays ubiquitous, overhead projector, defy detailed treatment and in the space available here examples only can be provided of the possibilities and potential of the principal audio and visual aids available to the busy teacher.

The tape recorder. Oral records of geographical experiences can be committed to tape and recorded for subsequent use in class. Recording of interviews with people from foreign countries, business people involved in locational decision-making, or local inhabitants relating environmental change in the locality, can all be undertaken by the teacher. Usually teachers have access to each of these at some time each year and teachers can often take advantage of the generosity of friends and neighbours with interesting stories to tell. Recorded on tape, and played back in class, these can prove useful and stimulating learning resources – though each interview should be kept relatively short. The beauty of the *recorded* interview is that it can be interrupted by the teacher should pupil attention begin to wane.

It is better, of course, if interviews are conducted by the pupils as part of a project or topic. Pupils can divide into teams to plan, direct, produce and participate in the interview. Simulated radio programmes can be produced on subjects like 'The changing village' or 'The local traffic problem'. The list of possible subjects is endless. Integration with work in English is an obvious context for such work to take place.

Records and music. The use of recorded music (on tape or disc) can be of great motivational value in geographical work. As part of regional geographical study, be it on parts of Britain or on regions of the world, regional music can provide an appreciation of a place different from that with which pupils are most familiar. In this way music can be used in association with artefacts of various kinds to provide children with insights into different cultures.

Table 6.4 Examples of the use of popular music in the geography lesson

Song title and performer	Exemplary lyric	Geographical idea illustrated
'Big Yellow Taxi' – Joni Mitchell	'They paved paradise And put up a parking lot . . . . They took all the trees and put them in a tree museum And they charged all the people A dollar and a half just to see 'em. . . . Hey farmer farmer Put away that DDT now Give me spots on my apples But leave me the birds and the bees.'	ecological degradation
'Detroit City' – Tom Jones (and many others)	'Last night I went to sleep in Detroit City And dreamed about those cotton fields back home . . .'	rural–urban migration; places in USA
'In the Ghetto' – Elvis Presley	'As the snow flies On a cold and grey Chicago morn A poor little baby child is born In the ghetto And his mother cries 'Cos if there's one thing that she don't need It's another hungry mouth to feed In the ghetto . . .'	the inner city; urban poverty
'Apeman' – The Kinks	'I think I'm sophisticated 'Cos I'm living my life Like a good homo sapien But all around me Everybody's multiplying And they're walking round like flies . . . So I'm no better than the animals Living in the cages of the zoo, man, 'Cos compared to the flowers And the birds and the trees I am an apeman . . . Oh what a life of luxury To be like an apeman . . .'	notions of 'development' and progress

In addition to this kind of application of music to geographical study the teacher can also use the lyrics of popular songs to illustrate a wide range of geographical ideas ranging from inner city problems to environmental degradation. Music is here used to stimulate involvement in certain themes rather than regions. The selection of examples will reflect the teacher's tastes and awareness of the current musical scene as those in Table 6.4 reflect those (and the age!) of the author. In using lyrics, it is useful to first play the song without reference to its subsequent use in teaching. Having played it once it can be repeated, this time with the prior instruction that the children should listen carefully to the words and attempt to interpret what the lyrics are about. The lyrics (or a selection deemed appropriate) can then be provided for the class to read and upon which a series of comprehension questions might be based.

Music can also be used in order to create geographical or environmental 'moods' for various lessons or topics. The Pastoral Symphony or Peer Gynt come first to mind though readers will undoubtedly be able to think of many more examples.

Video. The advent of both the video camera and the video cassette has created great possibilities for imaginative work in primary school geography. It is not that uncommon for schools to possess their own video camera and if one is available teachers should take full advantage of it to enliven their geographical work. Making short films of the locality, filming changes in the environment as they are happening and interviewing people of topical interest are all well worth doing with older children of primary age. Children can direct and take part in such productions, producing scripts and scenarios for themselves.

Commercially produced television films for geography are well known to most primary schools. Both the BBC and ITV are active in the production of educational films and those with a geographical slant are frequently shown in primary class-rooms. Teachers receive regular information on such produc-tions and often printed support material is produced with suggestions for accompanying work. The use of film as a child-minding device is tempting and the production of appropriate worksheets is necessary if the impact of the film is to be maximised.

Slides. Again, slides may be commercially produced or may be the result of the teacher's own photographic flair. In many ways slides are more manageable than strips; the latter contain too many slides for optimal impact and individual slides can be placed in the order desired by the teacher. It is probable that the optimal number of slides which should be used is no more than 10, since after this number the addition of more visual images produces diminishing returns in terms of learning. Carefully selected slides, chosen to make the desired impact, are important should this medium be selected for classroom use.

Computers in the primary geography classroom

Recent years have witnessed the rapid adoption of micro-computers in primary schools, the Department of Education and Science and local education authorities strongly supporting such innovation. In Britain the most frequently used machines appear to be the BBC model B and the RML 480Z. A considerable amount of commercially produced software now exists for these, and other, machines. Usually the primary school will contain only one or two micros and for this reason the teacher needs to be aware of the ways and contexts in which they can be used.

Basically the micro-computer is analogous to three well-known classroom resources. Firstly, we can think of the micro as being similar to the blackboard, i.e. to be used to display information to the entire class. Secondly, it can be compared to a reference book, i.e. when pupils want it they go to it and consult it. A third analogy which is less applicable to the primary school is the pencil analogy, i.e. where everybody has one. Tapsfield (1984a) suggests that there are four areas of computer assisted geographical work at this level. These are mapping skills, simulations, information handling, and spatial awareness. Each can be reviewed in turn.

Mapwork skills. According to Boardman (1985, 131) 'the microcomputer provides a versatile aid to enable children to practise and reinforce basic mapwork skills'. Most programs of this type are concerned with testing children's acquisition of skills such as using grid references or compass orientation. Map-work skills programs are considered useful because (i) they tackle an identifiable task in a simple way, (ii) they provide an entertaining way of acquiring what could easily become rather mundane skills with immediate reinforcement if the pupil is right or wrong, and (iii) they are often structured at a variety of levels. Particularly good examples are GRIDREF and, at a different level of geographical scale ATLAS, concerned respectively with working with grid references and, for older primary children, finding their way around an atlas. At the larger scale LANDMARK expects children to interpret an area shown on the screen in order to search for symbols of likely locations. GRIDREF, ATLAS, and LANDMARK are all found in Tapsfield (1984b).

Simulations. Decision-making skills can be enhanced by using computer simulations. Problem-solving, which may involve relatively elaborate numerical computation, can be easily handled by the computer, as can the keeping of records and accounts. Two examples of computer simulations give the flavour of such learning strategies. DAIRY enables pupils to locate a dairy in a least-cost location while MILL sets out to locate a windmill in a least-transport-cost location for a weight-losing industry. Other programs like TOWN PLANNER involve siting facilities in a town, while from physical geography UNDERSTANDING THE WEATHER simulates the weather as a system and helps children appreciate its dynamic elements.

Information handling. In primary school project work, topics and field work can generate substantial amounts of data and information. The micro-computer can store and manipulate such data to good effect. Perhaps the most well-known information-handling program is FACTFILE, which allows information on any topic (e.g. names, counties, countries, etc.) to be stored and interrogated. In addition to using information obtained from field work the micro-computer can create data bases from secondary sources such as censuses, reference books and maps.

Spatial awareness. The micro-computer can also help in the development of directional skills which will be required learning in mathematics (geometry) as well as geography. Computer-controlled toys such as Bigtrack can be programmed to go forward, left and right and as such can usefully reinforce directional concepts.

This section has served to alert the reader to the potential of the micro-computer in geographical work at the primary level. Further information can be found in Tapsfield (1984b) and on the regular computer page in the quarterly publication of the Geographical Association, *Teaching Geography*.

Simulations and games

Simulations form a large family of classroom activities which incorporate all things occurring under the label of 'let's pretend'. When an element of competition is introduced into simulations they become games. A pioneer of geographical gaming, Rex Walford (1969, 1981b), argues that games and simulations provide the following benefits. Firstly, they develop participation in group activities and the growth of social skills; secondly they involve practice in decision-making in a rational and considered manner, and thirdly they combine thinking and feeling about situations and problems. More specifically and geographically, (i) they seek to encourage the development of *empathy* with people from other places or from other environmental situations, (ii) they aim to assist the understanding of working processes (particularly decision-making processes) and systems, (iii) they contribute to the recognition of the interdisciplinary nature of most 'real-life' situations, and (iv) they are highly motivational aids to teaching. Simulations, games and role plays are best illustrated by actual examples; each broad type can be reviewed in turn.

Simulations can be typified by a fairly simple and relatively mechanical example based on an exercise found in *New Ways in Geography* (Cole and Beynon, 1968, 1982). It involves the child in simulating the route of a railway over a landscape of varied physical features (see Figure 6.5). In this example the aim is to show how physical factors influence the cost of railway construction, though in the final analysis it is

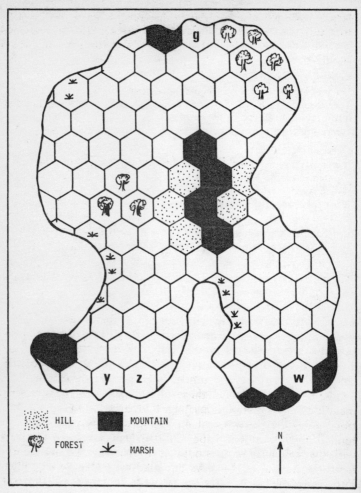

Railway builders

Three players are needed for this game. Each player needs about 20 counters, small enough to cover one hexagon on the board (see map).

Step 1 Each player pretends to be a railway building company, faced with the problem of building a railway from the south to the north of the island of Hexagonia shown on the map.

Player 1 starts building from Y; player 2 from Z and player 3 from W.

Step 2   Each player *in turn* puts a counter on a hexagon, starting from each player's base. Each player's aim is to get to hexagon G at the north of the island. Each player builds a railway from south to north across the map.

Rules

One counter is needed on a blank hexagon.

Two counters are needed to cover a hexagon with a hill, marsh or forest.

Four counters are needed on a hexagon with a mountain.

Questions

Which parts of the island were the most expensive (i.e. used the most counters) to build on?

Which were the cheapest to build on?

What other kinds of things, apart from railways, might follow these kinds of rules?

Can you think of any places *in the real world* which are like the island of Hexagonia?

Figure 6.5   A simple railway-building game
(After Cole and Beynon, 1969)

individuals who decide where the route actually goes. In other words, it adopts a probabilistic rather than deterministic position with regards to the influence of the environment. Crossing rivers and mountains impose additional costs; passing through mining towns or timber areas generate revenues.

Simulations other than those of a pencil-and-paper variety include computer simulations (page 124) and 'hardware' simulations involving the physical modelling of some aspect of the human or physical landscape. Children will have been familiar with the making of models out of cardboard and papier mâché from the infants school days and this work can be extended into geographical studies of a wide number of themes. However, less well known at the primary level is the way in which simulations can be used to illustrate *processes* which lead to features in the landscape. A series of such simulations has been reviewed by Chambers (1986) and relate to various aspects of glaciated landscapes. For example, the requirements for a simulation designed to show the way in which 'kettle holes' (depressions formed in glacial deposits by the melting of isolated blocks of buried ice) are formed are simply a sand tray,

Classroom styles

Jamaican Fisherman (worksheet for players)
Imagine you are a fisherman living in the village shown on the map.

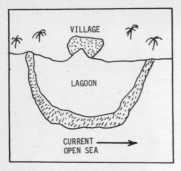

(After: R. Abler, J. Adams and P. Gould,
Spatial Organisation, Prentice Hall, 1971, 481)

Notice that your village faces out on to a lagoon which is a calm
stretch of water enclosed by a reef. Each day your fishing boat leaves
the village to catch fish in pots which are lowered from the fishing
canoes. The *BEST FISH* are caught in the *open sea*; those *in the
lagoon* are *poor quality*, fetching lower prices at the village fish
market. Now, the problem is that out at sea there is an occasional
current which batters the fishing pots on the sea beds so that the
fishermen catch no fish at all.

The fisherman's daily task is to decide where to locate his pots.
Should he put them all out at sea?
Should he put half of them in the lagoon?
Should he put them all in the lagoon?
These are the three choices open to him.

The following table shows how much money you would earn if you
were one of the fishermen. The table tells you how much you earn
depending on which strategy you adopt.

Table A

	Current	*No Current*
All pots in	17	11
In – Out	5	17
All pots out	–5	20

(Why will you lose money if you put all your pots out and there is a
current?)

128

Table B   *Record Sheet for 'Jamaican Fishermen'*

	Pot location	Current (Yes/No)	Day's Earnings
Monday			
Tuesday			
Wednesday			
Thursday			
Friday			
Monday			
Tuesday			
Wednesday			
Thursday			
Friday			
		This week's earnings:	

Notes for the teacher
STEPS IN PLAYING THE GAME

1 Ask children to select a location for Monday. Children enter location in column 1 of Table B.

2 The teacher throws a dice to determine whether there is a current or not.

   If 1, 2 or 3 is thrown there *is* a current; if 4 or 5 is thrown there is no current (6 is null). Children indicate 'YES' or 'NO' in column 2.

   N.B. The teacher *can* tell the class the probability of there being a current OR can leave the children to *learn* the probability of there being a current or not, through trial and error – as generations of real-live fishermen had to do!

3 Children enter daily earnings in column 3.

4 Play for 10 rounds (each round = 1 day; no fishing on Saturdays and Sundays).

5 Children work out their earnings for one fortnight and enter result in appropriate place.

6 Children look at record of their locational choices. They calculate how many times out of 10 they used each location. Teacher discusses different strategies, indicating that some children were risk-takers while others were more cautious.

   N.B. In reality 69% of the fishermen in a Jamaican village placed their pots *in* the lagoon and 31% placed them in the open sea.

Figure 6.6a   *Left:* 'Jamaican fishermen': worksheet for players. This game is suitable for pupils aged 10–11 and introduces them to situations where decision-makers have to operate in conditions of environmental uncertainty.   6.6b   *Above:* Teacher's notes for 'Jamaican Fishermen'.

some sand and some ice cubes. The sand in the tray represents the glacial deposit and the ice blocks, buried near the surface, represent blocks of stagnant ice. As the ice melts depressions are formed, a process analogous to that which happens in the real world.

Games are competitive simulations. The extent to which teachers place emphasis on the competitive nature of the game will depend on the individual. The emphasis placed on winning need not be excessive. An example of a game used to illustrate the influence of physical geography on human decision-making and suitable for use with classes of 10–11-year-olds is shown in Figure 6.6. The central characteristic of this game is the 'pay-off matrix', a core concept in game theory and the basis for any game involving two or more 'actors'. In the case described in Figure 6.6 the Jamaican fishermen are 'playing a game' against the environment. The fishermen have three possible strategies – to put all their fishing pots inside the lagoon, all outside or half inside and half outside. The environment, on the other hand, has two strategies – to produce a current outside the lagoon which damages the fishing pots or not to have a current. Greater clarification will be obtained by working through the worksheets (Figure 6.6b).

Role-play is at the more child-centred end of the games–simulation spectrum and can border closely on drama. Essentially, the role play is a variant on the class debate in a geographical context. We have already come close to describing a roleplay in our discussion of local problem-solving in Chapter 4. In setting up a geographical role-play the teacher identifies a situation in which more than one or two perceptions or attitudes exist. Any local or distant issue will do; headlines such as 'Which route for the by-pass?' or 'The Olympics for Birmingham' can form the stimulus for the development of excellent role-plays. An example is provided as Figure 6.7. In this pupils assume the roles of different residents of a hypothetical village in Colorado faced with the possibility of the Winter Olympic Games being sited in their valley. The worksheet makes the situation clear. The children, working in pairs, prepare a case for each person. They then have to decide which one of them will put the viewpoint of that person to a simulated meeting of the local community. Different perceptions of the same situation will invariably emerge; some will

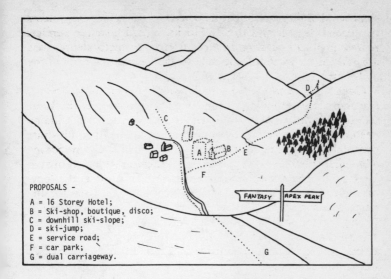

PROPOSALS -

A = 16 Storey Hotel;
B = Ski-shop, boutique, disco;
C = downhill ski-slope;
D = ski-jump;
E = service road;
F = car park;
G = dual carriageway.

Winter Olympics for Fantasy Valley?
In Colorado USA, lies the small mountain village of Fantasy, located in the beautiful Fantasy Valley. People in the village are very excited because they have just heard that there is a plan to hold the Winter Olympic Games in their valley. This would have a great impact on the village and many new buildings, roads and other facilities would have to be built. The people described below decide to meet at the local bar to discuss this. (You can invent other people if you like).

Sandy James: 22 years old, lives at Fantasy and very keen on skiing. Works as a secretary in Blackwall, 40 km away.

Paul Barry: 40 years old. Road engineer; lives in Fantasy.

Lois Maxwell: Runs a small hotel in Fantasy.

Gail Hartshorne: 25 years old; tourist from New York. Has visited Apex Peak and found the hotel there very expensive.

Steve Lobeck: age 50; runs the Apex Peak hotel 20 km from Fantasy.

Bill Baggett: age 67; has a small farm in Fantasy Valley and has worked it for the last 40 years.

Nora Semple: age 60; a tourist from Boston; very keen bird watcher, she has visited Fantasy for the past 27 years.

Figure 6.7   Worksheet for role-playing simulation

131

Figure 6.8 Cartoon to accompany role-play. Children fill in the bubbles as part of a de-briefing activity
(Based on an idea in DEC, 1985)

welcome the Winter Olympics; others will not. The teacher will act as chairman and if so desired will act as the final arbitrator in the debate, deciding what the community as a whole feels about the proposal. Alternatively, the class could take a vote on how they feel they should respond to the proposal. (Pupils might be interested to know that in reality the state of Colorado decided *not* to bid for the Winter Olympics in the 1970s on the grounds that the event would generate too much traffic and congestion.)

Following this role-play a useful exercise is to establish whether pupils can transfer what they have learnt to different situations. A cartoon of a public meeting can be presented with empty 'bubbles' coming from the mouths of members of the audience (Figure 6.8) and the children are asked to fill them in with different perspectives on the viewpoint presented from the platform.

A crucial thing to bear in mind when using games and simulations of the kinds described above is that they should be used as learning activities rather than simply entertainment or child-minding resources. They should obviously be set in some curricular context – the role play described above might have formed part of a work unit on 'winter'; the Jamaican Fisherman game part of a unit on 'fishing'. Furthermore, it is essential that a de-briefing session is devoted to reinforcing the points or key ideas that are expected to be learnt. In the case of the fishing game, for example, the teacher is less likely to want to teach children that pots are used to catch fish in Jamaica than to make the point that decisions are being made in situations of environmental uncertainty and to provoke pupils into establishing parallel situations elsewhere (e.g. farmers in Britain).

Walford and Taylor (1972) recognise at least three ways in which role-plays or simulations can be slotted into a unit of work. The simulation could be the centrepiece of the unit, preceded by preparatory work and briefing and followed by de-briefing and follow-up work. Alternatively the simulation could be used as an initial stimulus to a work unit, with a short initial briefing on the simulation and afterwards a more substantial period of explanation, stimuli and follow-up work. A third alternative involves using the simulation twice in order to allow players to reflect on, or improve, their performance. The individual teacher and the particular subject or situation will determine which of these approaches are used.

Games and simulations are powerful motivational teaching and learning strategies. A large number of examples can be found in books devoted to geographical work at the primary level (e.g. Mills, 1981; Catling *et al.*, 1981) and teachers should have little difficulty in designing their own materials (Fien *et al.*, 1985) given the examples provided in this section.

Topic work

We have already emphasised the widespread use of topics in primary schools (page 2) and it is now appropriate to consider ways in which we can ensure that a geographical dimension is included within them. Before doing so, however, it will be germane to briefly review the rationale for the topic approach.

Topics originated as an attempt to develop all-round education, recognising the artificiality of subject-boundaries. Essentially a humanistic form of education, topics are supposed to grow out of the interests of the child; the teacher is seen as a consultant or provider of resources rather than a pedagogue. Disciplinary boundaries, it is argued, serve to obscure, rather than encourage the awareness of, 'reality'.

However, despite its common usage, the topic approach is open to a number of criticisms. Her Majesty's Inspectorate (DES, 1978) criticised topics as being overconcerned with children using low-order skills like simple and mindless copying. There also existed a mismatch between what children would have reasonably been capable of doing and what they were actually involved in. Frequently topic work has been found to be fragmented and superficial.

A problem arises for those teachers espousing the topic approach in that a decision has to be made about the kind of structure which is imposed upon the work to be undertaken. It might be argued that 'structure' and child-centredness are incompatible, but this view can be countered with the assertion that 'totally unstructured experience is no experience at all' (Bonnett, 1986). All meaningful experience needs at least some sense of order.

Table 6.5 Different kinds of structure in topic work

	Type of structure	Source of content
Pre-specification	Teacher-centred	Teacher's personal view of content
	Knowledge-centred	Geography as a source of content
	Skill-centred	Project as vehicle for learning skills
More open	Problem-centred	A local or distant problem
	Child-centred	The child's own consciousness

Bonnett (1986) suggests that five 'structuring principles' can be applied to topic work. These are shown in Table 6.5. Each approach is meant not to be mutually exclusive and are intended to serve as models of how topic work might be organised. At one end of the 'structure scale' is the teacher-centred structure which would involve the pre-specification of both content and learning outcomes, the teacher deciding what would be included. If the teacher was a geographer, particular knowledge-centred questions might form the basis for the topic. We have already seen, in Table 4.1, some of the *geographical* approaches to many topics and Bennetts (1985) has provided a shorter list made up of:

- where is it located?
- what area does it serve?
- how far is it to various parts of the area it serves?
- how long does it take to get to (or from) these places?
- where are its nearest neighbours? What is the distribution?
- what sort of places does it serve?
- what routes are taken to reach it?

Such questions could obviously be applied to a wide variety of popular themes. The fire-station, the corner shop, the super-market, the football club, the park, etc. Although somewhat 'spatial' in character, this shortlist at least ensures a minimum amount of geographical content.

Moving down Table 6.5, we come to two approaches which are more open in their degree of specification. Structure may, in the case of the problem-centred approach, be provided by the enquiry itself. The content will depend to an extent on where the enquiry leads, though it is unlikely to lead *anywhere* because of the constraints on information and resources available to the child and because of the ideological back-ground in which upbringing and education is rooted. Finally, at the most open end of the spectrum we have the truly child-centred approach in which the topic is based on children's own felt needs and concerns. Individual teachers will respond to this approach in different ways, having to decide how far the children themselves can *initiate* their own topics, the extent to which such choice might be *negotiated*, and the degree to which teachers will act as *consultants*.

The point being made here is that structure need not be excessive. If we consider a topic on say, a bar of chocolate (Figure 6.9), differently imposed structures could be located at different parts of the topic web. A geographer might stress the spatial aspects of the web, e.g. communications and transport. A child-centred approach could potentially include all, and more, aspects of the web shown in Figure 6.9.

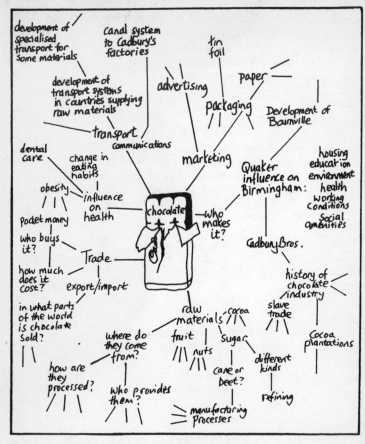

Figure 6.9   Topic web from 'A Bar of Chocolate'
(After DEC, 1985)

Using their imagination

Children's imaginations can be further harnessed in geographical work by incorporating art, poetry and drama into subjects of a geographical character. Artwork can be utilised, for example, in the design of posters ranging in subject matter from caring for the environment to advertising a town for the benefit of prospective holidaymakers or industrialists. In such cases the *geographical* content of the subject under consideration should be stressed. Likewise, children can use their imagination to create newspaper front pages with news items dealing with geographical events. Pretending to be a reporter at the scene of a flood, earthquake or avalanche, for example, provides not only an opportunity for the development of writing skills, but also a chance for the teacher to establish the extent to which geographical subject matter has been appreciated.

Likewise, writing skills can be incorporated with geographical awareness in poetry. Consider the example shown here which is a poem written by a 10-year-old boy on the subject of water. Not only does he display a sensitive poetic style, but also an awareness of certain terms used in river study, the 'stages' of a river's long profile and the hydrological cycle.

> A windswept marsh,
> The source of a river,
> Soggy and dank,
> The quagmire deep,
> Slowly seeping, slowly drifting.
>
> We come across a waterfall,
> Wet and wild,
> Warm and mild,
> Shimmering bright,
> Frantic and feverish,
> Running fast,
> Infinite life.
>
> In a hurry to get away,
> So, down, down to the river,
> Down, down to the sea,
> Down, down 'til we come to the estuary.
>
> Up, up to the clouds,
> Up, up on high,
> Up, up to the very top of the sky.
>
> Anthony Paul, aged 10

Conclusion

The varied ingredients which go to make a 'good teacher' are ill defined and unclear. Assessment of teachers by their pupils, their peers and their headteachers may differ considerably since the criteria used will vary between and within such groups, partly as a result of their educational base positions (see Chapter 2).

Personality, careful preparation, subject expertise, enthusiasm, care and consideration may all be important constituents of the good teacher's make-up. This chapter has stressed that a variety of approaches might be adopted in geographical teaching. These approaches have been seen to range from teacher-centred to pupil-centred strategies. A variety of classroom approaches is deemed desirable at all educational levels. This chapter has demonstrated that at the primary level a very wide range of teaching strategies can be utilised by teachers who wish to bring a varied diet of geographical fare to their children's educational menu.

Further reading

David Mills (ed.), *Geographical Work in Primary and Middle Schools*, The Geographical Association, Sheffield, 1981.

Roger Cracknell, 'Geography through topics in primary and middle schools', *Teaching Geography Occasional Papers*, 31, 1979.

7

Towards a geographical education

This chapter attempts to draw together some of the threads presented in the previous pages and begins to move towards ways in which geographical work in the primary school might be structured. We have already stressed (in Chapter 2) that curriculum development includes the selection of content, a choice of learning strategies and the teacher's evaluation. The kinds of skills, resources, topics and approaches to map work, local study and the consideration of more distant places was contained in subsequent chapters. It is now time to consider how content should be structured in terms of progression and ask what skills and what facts are appropriate for young children to have learnt at different stages during the primary phase.

A spiral approach

This is not the place to discuss whether geography is taught as a separate subject or whether it should be included as part of one of a variety of integrated approaches. Assuming that geographical work is undertaken at the primary level, the question we pose here is how it can be organised. In organising the geographical content of primary school work, it should be recognised that some kind of *progression* is required. 'Ideally, a programme should be designed to facilitate progression in learning by building systematically on pupils' previous experience and achievements' (Bennetts, 1985, 160). We have strongly stressed this in our discussion about map work, learning about the locality and learning about more distant places, emphasising that it is from children's private geographies that more formal geographical education should build. It is also essential, of course, to match children's learning experiences to their intellectual capabilities. Catling (1978a) has suggested that the core geographical concepts of location, distribution and relationships in space could be linked to children's evolving conception of space (i.e. from topological to euclidean, see page 14). For example, in teaching ideas about, say, spatial relationships, the focus of the teacher's attention in the early years will be on everyday spatial relationships, building on children's private geographies. By the end of the primary years, however, the child will have been introduced to spatial relationships at regional, national and international scales. The crucial point, therefore, is that geography 'should seek to harness the child's evolving spatial conception in developing curriculum objectives' (Catling, 1978a, 27) (see Figure 7.1).

Perhaps the major influence on progression in the geography curriculum has been the work of Jerome Bruner (1963) whose highly readable book, *The Process of Education* stimulated a number of geographical educators to experiment with what has become known as the spiral curriculum. Essentially, Bruner

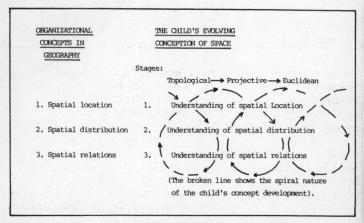

Figure 7.1 The relationship between the fundamental concepts of geography and spatial concept development in the child: overview of the structure
(Source: Catling, 1978a, 27)

suggested that 'our schools may be wasting precious years by postponing the teaching of many important subjects on the ground that they are too difficult . . . the foundations of any subject may be taught to anybody at any stage in some form' (Bruner, 1963, 12). He went on to add that the basic ideas of any subject which were central to it should be revised continually, broadening and deepening them. This spiral curriculum was justified on two counts. Firstly, it provided a *structure* for the subject and secondly, and as a result, learning was made easier.

It may surprise some readers to assert that ideas taught in universities could be introduced to primary school children, as Bruner suggests. However, let us take one example from human geography and show how it is quite possible for an idea initially introduced into the 'academic' literature to be presented to primary school children.

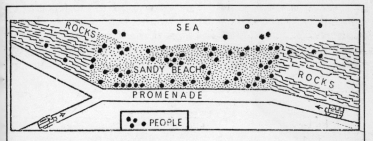

On this map there is a sandy beach between the sea and the promenade. There are many people on the beach and they are shown by large dots (●). Mr Block the ice cream seller comes quite early to park *on the promenade*. He wants to sell as many ice creams as possible to the people on the beach.

Exercise
Mark on the map in your workpad with a X where you think Mr. Block will park.
Later in the day Mr Brick, another ice cream seller, arrives in his van. Mark with an O where you think he will park. Do you think Mr Block and Mr Brick might agree on the best places for each to be?

Figure 7.2 The classical mathematical problem of spatial equilibrium in a linear market – for 9-year-olds!
(Source: Cole and Beynon, 1968)

In 1929 an article was published in the *Economic Journal* called 'Stability in Competition' which considered the problem of best location for both a monopolist and for duopolists on a linear market (Hotelling, 1929). This problem has subsequently been called the 'ice cream salesman problem' for reasons which will be obvious from Figure 7.2. This is taken from *New Ways in Geography* and shows how Cole and Beynon (1969) presented the problem to 8- or 9-year-olds. Clearly it *is* possible to present ideas at different levels of sophistication.

The widespread publicity afforded Bruner's work coincided with the interest shown by geographers in the re-emergence of the spatial tradition in the subject (see page 4) and their attempt to identify fundamental spatial concepts which would provide a structure for their subject (Haggett, 1965). The spatial concepts of points, hierarchies, surfaces, movements, networks and diffusion provided a geographical structure for Bruner's spiral curriculum. The relevance of this to teaching in the primary school was that a matrix could theoretically be constructed with the concepts providing the headings for the columns and the age levels being the identification for the rows (see Figure 7.3). Everson (1973) presents this matrix as a way of operationalising the spiral curriculum, suggesting that all that is now required is the design of work units for each of the boxes.

However, little agreement exists on *what* exactly the key concepts of the subject are which can form the headings for each of the columns. Instead, teachers have tended to take

		CONCEPTS			
	Concept 1	Concept 2	Concept 3	Concept 4	Concept n
Level n					
Level 3					
Level 2					
Level 1					

LEVELS

Figure 7.3　The notion of the spiral curriculum. Learning units on each concept need to be fitted into each cell of the matrix
(After an idea by Everson, 1973, 60)

particular topics (e.g. rivers, farming, forests) or particular skills (e.g. map work, behaviour) and identify what might be appropriately taught at different ages. A spiral approach to geographical work on deserts and housing, for example, is shown in Table 7.1.

Table 7.1   The spiral curriculum applied to two topics. (after ILEA, 1981, 4)

Topics		
Age	Deserts	Housing
12	Examining some contemporary responses to the challenge of desert environments, e.g. irrigation schemes, tourism, oil	Investigation of the evolution of the local landscape. What was there before the houses? Use of old maps and pictures
9	Looking at some traditional ways in which people have adapted to living in desert conditions	Simple classification of houses according to type: terraced, detached, semi-detached, etc. Use of symbols and colours on maps and sections. Designing the ideal house
6	Learning about plants and animals in the desert; looking at and making pictures and models. How do things survive in the desert?	Drawing individual and imaginary homes; labelling roof, door, chimney, window, etc.

In terms of graphicacy skills Boardman (1983) has provided a helpful list of what might be appropriate for pupils of differnt year-groups. Obviously these are *average* abilities and a considerable range of competences will exist within any year group. Table 7.2 should be related back to many of the things discussed in Chapter 3 on mapping skills.

Just as mapping skills can be tabulated in such a way, teachers can also work towards planning a curriculum in geography which involves the identification of abilities in other areas. For example, a group of teachers from Oxfordshire

Table 7.2 Mapping skills at different ages

5–7

By the age of 7 children should normally be able to:

1   Follow directions using left, right, forwards, in a circle, etc.
2   Describe the relative locations of objects using before, behind, in front of, to the left of, etc.
3   Sort objects by relative size and draw round them.
4   Sort objects by their shape, such as squares, circles, etc. and draw round them.
5   Draw round life size objects such as coins, pencils, toys, etc. to show their shapes in plan form.
6   Draw routes between objects drawn, such as the path of an imaginary crawling insect.
7   Draw symbols to illustrate picture maps or imaginary maps.
8   Measure spaces between objects using hands or feet.

7–9

By the age of 9 children should normally be able to:

9   Plot the cardinal directions NESW.
10   Use a compass to find NESW in the school playground.
11   Draw a plan at a very large scale, such as a desk top with objects on it.
12   Measure from a large scale plan, such as a teacher-prepared plan of the classroom.
13   Insert in their approximate positions on the plan objects in the room, such as blackboard, cupboards.
14   Record around the plan features seen from the room, such as playground, trees.
15   Draw free-hand a map showing a simple route, such as the journey to school.
16   Make a simple model of part of the neighbourhood such as a row of shops.
17   Give locations in grid squares, such as A1, B3, etc. as on an A to Z road map.
18   Measure straight line distances between two points on an A to Z road map.
19   Draw some conventional symbols on an imaginary map and add a key.
20   Identify different countries shown on atlas maps.

9–11

By the age of 11 children should normally be able to:

21 Plot the sixteen points of the compass.
22 State bearings in degrees: 45, 90, 135, etc.
23 Indicate directions in the neighbourhood.
24 Align a map of the school and neighbourhood by means of compass and buildings, e.g. church, numbered houses.
25 Find directions and bearings using a compass.
26 Orientate a large scale map (1:1,250 or 1:2,500) using buildings as reference points.
27 Relate position on the ground to location on a large scale map.
28 Use grid lines to locate points.
29 Give four figure grid references using eastings and northings.
30 Draw a plan of the classroom and/or school building.
31 Identify and name rooms on a teacher-prepared plan of the school.
32 Make measurements on large scale maps of the local area (1:1,250 or 1:2,500 or 1:10,000).
33 Measure the straight line distance between two fixed points on maps of progressively smaller scales.
34 Measure the winding distance along roads between two fixed points on maps of progressively smaller scales.
35 Compare symbols for the same feature on maps of progressively smaller scales.
36 Realise that the degree of generalisation on maps increases with decreasing scale.
37 Appreciate that some symbols on smaller scale maps are disproportionate to the size of the objects they represent.
38 Identify features on a low level oblique aerial photograph of the local area.
39 Make a scale model of part of the local area showing roads and buildings.
40 Give locations on atlas maps using latitude and longitude.

(Source: Boardman, 1983)

145

produced a list of children's attitudes and values *and* behaviour and action which they felt would be appropriate for the lower and upper junior school stages. Though the geographical nature of such ideas is not immediately obvious, the notions of justice, tolerance, sharing and caring do clearly have geographical implications, for example, caring about the environment, tolerance of other cultures' ideas. More controversially, perhaps, the teachers concerned also list appropriate behaviour and action, arising out of attitudes and values which have been taught. These may not immediately appear too problematic, but one can imagine some parental reaction to 10-year-olds wanting to 'make a case in public in relation to a local or contemporary issue' (Table 7.3), for example.

If such 'spiral' approaches can be used to structure progression in content, skills, attitudes, behaviours and actions they should surely also be able to accommodate the progressive accumulation of *factual* knowledge. At the lower end of the primary school children will be concerned with the acquisition of factual knowledge and of terminology which are related to the local area. In due course, national place-name knowledge will be part of the spatial framework within which enquiry takes place and the nation's linkages with the world will further expand the child's range of awareness. There is no definitive checklist of place names and locations with which children of different stages should be aware. To some extent, the map work series *Mapstart* (Catling, 1986) provides an indication of the size threshold of places for which it is reasonable for children to know the approximate location. Assuming that teachers agree that it is impossible to know the location of everything, emphasis should initially be placed on familiarising children with the key places in the immediate locality, the same principle being applied as we move up the school in relation to the country and then to the world. Such 'key places' will usually be determined by their significance to the lives of the children in the class, irrespective of scale, but more important is the learned ability to find out where places are, should the need arise.

This chapter has suggested that the spiral approach is a satisfactory way of structuring progression within the geography curriculum. With exemplification from classroom materials, we have highlighted the fact that basic elements of geography can be introduced, *à la* Bruner, at an early age. The reinforcement of these ideas, in differing and more sophisticated situations, not only provides a structure for the geography curriculum but, more importantly, aids children's learning.

Table 7.3   Suggested attitudes, values, behaviour and actions for primary school pupils. (Source: Fyson, 1984, 60)

Children's attitudes and values	Children's behaviour; action
Age range 7+ to 9+ ('Lower junior') (a) *Justice* – valuing 'fairness'; belief in 'reward'. (b) *Tolerance* – from self to others; willingness to try what is strange. (c) *Sharing* – being able to share with others. (d) *Caring* – simple care for others and for one's surroundings. (e) *Appreciation* – enjoying things from other countries and cultures. (f) *Self-confidence* – feeling of ability to reach objectives.	(a) Simple direct actions arising from previous sections: e.g. handling conflicts; caring for others in class and family, and for local environment. (b) Simple caring for others further away: e.g. knitting blankets (squares) for refugees; small-scale fund-raising.
9+ to 11+ ('Upper junior') (a) *Justice* as applied between groups. (b) *Tolerance* – group tolerance; readiness to accept differences between cultures. (c) *Sharing* – valuing the ideal of sharing; sharing between groups. (d) *Caring* – developing feelings of responsibility towards others and the environment. Reasons for caring. (e) *Appreciation* – enjoying differences between cultures. (f) *Self-confidence* – in a minority; taking responsibility; 'going solo'.	(a) Organising programmes to care for one's own school and local environment; maintaining them in a clean and safe condition; making improvements. (b) Organising and improving relationships between one's own people and other groups; e.g. parents, old people, minorities, other communities, people in difficulties. Day visits and exchanges with them. (c) Exchanging information with a different culture overseas. (d) Making a case in public in relation to a local or contemporary issue.

8

Conclusion and on going further

Geographical work in the primary school has vast scope and potential for achieving broad educational aims. At the same time it is today recognised that geographical aims and objectives are themselves central targets for teachers during the primary phase. Among the skills pupils need to have acquired by the end of the primary school years are those relating to the elements of map work, location, direction, orientation, etc. Possession of such skills will not only make the transition to secondary school easier; it will also make learning in the primary school more rigorous and less subject to the kinds of criticisms voiced on the first pages of this book.

Geographical learning starts as soon as a child begins to move about and children arrive at school with their own private views of the world. We have suggested that we are in no way initiating children to subjects that are new and that there is a case to be made for the building of learning situations on to the extra-mural experiences of children derived from friends, parents, media and so on. Often, we are forced – through the desire to produce a more balanced learning environment (Stradling *et al.*, 1984, 6) – to provide different geographies from those of the vernacular variety which our pupils already possess.

Individual teachers will be the best people to decide on the precise nature of the geographical content of their day-to-day work, be it in topic or disciplinary form. However, mapping skills form a basic element of graphicacy in which all primary children should be well-versed by the age of 11. Much map work, and indeed, other studies, can be rooted in the locality of the school. More distant places, too, can be introduced by means of initially identifying their links with the local area.

Between the chalk and talk of the didactic teaching style and the 'free drama' of the humanistic teacher exist a range of teaching and learning styles, each of which can find a place in the teacher's battery of classroom skills. The 'good story well told' need not necessarily be rejected; but a whole range of other resources, ranging from the well-chosen text through the current pop record to the local newspaper and colour supplement can all be used to help geography be an enjoyable and worthwhile subject. The newer media of film, video and computer all have their place, but so too do the more traditional methods of art, poetry and drama, all set in geographical situations of course.

It is impossible in the space available in this book to describe all the possible sources of ideas for geographical work in the primary school. The bibliography will provide a useful source of further references, but all teachers with more than a passing interest in geographical education should join the Geographical Association (343 Fulwood Road, Sheffield), which publishes many materials appropriate for work at the primary level. In particular its quarterly journal, *Teaching Geography*, contains many useful classroom ideas. The same can be said about the *Bulletin of Environmental Education* (produced by Streetwork, Notting Dale Urban Studies Centre, Notting Dale, London). In addition, foreign journals like the American *Journal of Geography* and the Australian *Geographical Education* have many helpful ideas of relevance to teachers all over the world. More recently the British *Contemporary Issues in Geography and Education* has emerged as a more radical (see page 32) alternative, serving to highlight the ideological basis of much school geography and providing exemplary teaching ideas. If teachers themselves cannot obtain each of these publications for their schools they should press their local geography adviser to purchase them for teachers' centres or resource bases.

Bibliography

Anderson, J., 1985, 'Teaching map skills; an inductive approach', *Journal of Geography*, 4, 1–4.

Bain, I., 1984, 'Will Arno Peters take over the world?', *The Geographical Magazine*, July.

Balchin, W. and Coleman, A., 1965, 'Graphicacy should be the fourth ace in the pack', *Times Educational Supplement*, Nov. 5th. (reprinted in Bale *et al.*, 1974, 78–86).

Bale, J., Graves, N. and Walford, R. (eds), 1974, *Perspectives on Geographical Education*, Oliver & Boyd, Edinburgh.

Ball, J., 1972, 'Towards a humanistic teaching of geography', in Helburn, 1972.

Barker, E., 1974, *Geography and Younger Children*, ULP, London.

Bassey, M., 1978, *Nine Hundred Primary School Teachers*, NFER, Oxford.

Bennetts, T., 1985, 'Geography from 5 to 16; a view from the inspectorate', *Geography*, 70, 4, 299–314.

Bishop, G. and Foulsham, J., 1973, *Children's Images of Harwich*, Working Paper, 3, Kingston Polytechnic School of Architecture.

Björklid, P., 1982, *Children's Outdoor Environment*, Gleerup, Lund.

Blades, M. and Spencer, D., 1986, 'Map use by young children', *Geography*, 71, 1, 47–52.

Blaut, J. and Stea, D., 1974, 'Mapping at the age of three', *Journal of Geography*, 73, 5–9.

Bloom, B. (ed.), 1956, *Taxonomy of Educational Objectives*, Longman, London.

Board, D., 1967, 'Maps as models', in Chorley, R. and Haggett, P. (eds), *Models in Geography*, Methuen, London, 671–719.

Boardman, D., 1983, *Graphicacy and Geography Teaching*, Croom Helm, London.

Boardman, D., 1985a, 'Spatial concept development in primary school mapwork', in Boardman, 1985b.

Boardman, D., 1985b (ed.), *New Directions in Geographical Education*, Falmer, Brighton.

Boardman, D., 1986 (ed.), *Handbook for Geography Teachers*, Geographical Association, Sheffield.

Boardman, D. and Towner, E., 1979, 'Reading Ordnance Survey maps: some problems of graphicacy', Faculty of Education, University of Birmingham.

Bonnett, M., 1986, 'Child centredness and the problem of structure in project work', *Cambridge Journal of Education*, 16, 1, 3–6.

Bowles, R., 1981, 'Physical geography: water and land in the local environment', in Mills, 1981, 38–48.

Bruner, J., 1963, *The Process of Education*, Random House, New York.

Bunge, W., 1965, 'Racism in geography', *The Crisis*, 2, 8, (reprinted in *Contemporary Issues in Geography and Education*, 1984, 1, 2, 10–11).

Burgess, J., 1974, 'Stereotyping and urban images', *Area*, 6, 3, 167–71.

Butler, J. *et al.*, 1984, *Moving into Maps*, Heinemann, London.

Carnie, J., 1972, 'Children's attitudes to other nationalities', in Graves, 1972, 121–34.

Catling, S., 1978a, 'The child's spatial conception and geographical education', *Journal of Geography*, 77, 1, 24–8.

Catling, S., 1978b, 'Cognitive mapping exercises as a primary geographical experience', *Teaching Geography*, 3, 120–3.

Catling, S., 1979, 'Whither primary geography?', *Teaching Geography*, 5, 2, 73–6.

Catling, S., 1981, 'Using maps and aerial photographs', in Mills, 1981.

Catling, S., 1986, *Mapstart*, 3 vols, Collins-Longman, London.

Catling, S. and Coleman, A., 1981, *Patterns on the Map; Introductory Booklet*, The Geographical Association, Sheffield.

Catling, S., Firth, T. and Rowbottom, D., 1981, *Outset Geography*, 4 vols, Oliver & Boyd, Edinburgh.

Chambers, W., 1986, 'Kettles, kames and kitchens', *Teaching Geography*, 11, 4, 164–5.

Charlton, W. and Bentley, J., 1983, *Finding out about Villages*, Batsford, London.

Cole, J.P. and Beynon, N., 1969, 1982, *New Ways in Geography*, 4 vols, Blackwell, Oxford.

Cole, J.P. and King, C., 1968, *Quantitative Geography*, Wiley, London.

Cole, J. and Whysall, P., 1968, 'Places in the news', *Bulletin of Quantitative Data for Geographers*, 17.

Connolly, J., 1986, 'Geography, development education and equal opportunities', *ILEA Geography Bulletin*, 23, 29.

Bibliography

Connor, C., 1976, 'Geography in the middle schools', *Teaching Geography*, 1, 178–82.

Cracknell, R., 1976, 'Geography in junior schools', *Geography*, 61.

Cracknell, R., 1979, 'Geography through topics in primary and middle schools', *Teaching Geography Occasional Papers*, 31.

Derricott, R., *et al.*, 1977, *Time, Place and Society; 8–13; Themes in Outline*, Collins, London.

DEC (Development Education Centre, Birmingham), 1985, *People Before Places*, DEC, Birmingham.

DES, 1974, *School Geography in the Changing Curriculum*, HMSO, London.

DES, 1978, *Primary Education in England*, HMSO, London.

Everson, J., 1973, 'The organisation of content; a suggested basis', in Walford, 1973, 181–6.

Fien, J., 1983, 'Humanistic geography', in Huckle, 1983.

Fien, J., Gerber, R. and Wilson, P. (eds), 1985, *The Geography Teacher's Guide to the Classroom*, Macmillan, Melbourne.

Fien, J., Hodginson, J. and Herschell, R., 1985, 'Using games and simulations in the geography classroom', in Fien, Gerber and Wilson, 1985, 111–22.

Firth, T., 1981, 'Weather studies', in Mills, 1981, 19–37.

Fisher, S. and Hicks, D. (eds), 1985, *World Studies 8–13: a Teachers Handbook*, Oliver & Boyd, Edinburgh.

Fyson, N. (ed.), 1984, *The Development Puzzle*, Hodder & Stoughton/CWDE, Sevenoaks.

Fyson, T. and Ward, C., 1973, *Streetwork*, London, Routledge & Kegan Paul.

Gerber, R., 1985, 'Developing graphics for effective learning', *Geographical Education*, 5, 1, 27–33.

Gill, D., 1983, 'Anti-racist education: of what relevance in the geography curriculum?', *Contemporary Issues in Geography and Education*, 1, 1, 6–19.

Gill, D., 1984, 'Studying maps', *Contemporary Issues in Geography and Education*, 1, 2, 33.

Goodey, B., 1971, *Perception of the Environment*, Occasional Paper 17, Centre for Urban and Regional Studies, University of Birmingham.

Gould, P., 1972, 'The black boxes of Jönköping', in Downs, R. and Stea, D. (eds), *Cognitive Mapping: Images of Spatial Environment*, Aldine, Chicago.

Gould, P. and White, R., 1974, *Mental Maps*, Penguin, Harmondsworth.

Graves, N., 1971, 'Objectives in teaching particular subjects', *Bulletin of the University of London Institute of Education*, 23.

Graves, N. (ed.), 1972, *New Movements in the Study and Teaching of*

Geography, Temple Smith, London.

Graves, N., 1979, *Curriculum Planning in Geography*, Heinemann, London.

Graves, N. (ed.), 1982, *New UNESCO Sourcebook for Geography Teaching*, UNESCO/Longman, London.

Haggett, P., 1965, *Locational Analysis in Human Geography*, Arnold, London.

Hart, R., 1979, *Children's Experience of Place*, Irvington, New York.

Helburn, N. (ed.), 1972, *Challenge and Change in College Geography*, AAG, Boulder.

Hill, D., 1972, 'Geography and geographic education; paradigms and prospects', in Helburn, 1972, 17–40.

Hirst, P., 1965, 'Liberal Education and the nature of knowledge', in Archambault (ed.), 1965, *Philosophical Analysis of Education*, Routledge, London.

Hotelling, H., 1929, 'Stability in Competition', *Economic Journal*, 39.

Huckle, J. (ed.), 1983, *Geographical Education; Reflection and Action*, OUP, Oxford.

ILEA, 1981, *The Study of Places in the Primary School*, ILEA, London.

Institute of Race Relations, 1982a, *Roots of Racism*, IRR, London.

Institute of Race Relations, 1982b, *Patterns of Racism*, IRR, London.

Jahoda, G., 1963, 'The development of children's ideas about country and locality', *British Journal of Educational Psychology*, 33.

Joseph, K., 1985, 'Geography in the school curriculum', *Geography*, 70, 4, 290–8.

Kemp, J., 1971, *Instructional Design*, Fearon, London.

Kohn, C., 1982, 'Real problem solving', in Graves, 1982.

Kropotkin, P., 1913, 'Decentralisation, integration of labour and human education', in Peet, R. (ed.), 1978, *Radical Geography*, Methuen, London.

Ladd, F., 1967, 'A note on the world across the street', *Harvard Graduate School of Education Association Bulletin*, 12, 47–8 (quoted in Gould and White, 1974).

Lead, P., 1987, *History in the Primary School*, Routledge & Kegan Paul, London.

Lines, C., 1971, *Teaching Environmental Studies in the Primary and Middle Schools*, Ginn, London.

Lines, C., 1984, *Teaching Environmental Studies in Primary and Middle Schools*, Ginn, London.

Manson, G. and Ridd, M. (eds), 1977, *New Perspectives on Geographic Education*, Kendall/Hunt, Dubuque, Iowa.

Manson, G. and Vuicich, G., 1977, 'Toward geographic literacy; objectives for geographic education in the primary school', in Manson and Ridd, 1977, 191–210.

Bibliography

Martin, F., 1986, 'Producing resource sheets', in Boardman, 1985b, 96–101.

Matthews, H., 1984, 'Cognitive mapping abilities of young boys and girls', *Geography*, 69, 4, 327–36.

Matthews, H., 1986, 'Children as map makers', *The Geographical Magazine*, March.

Maye, B., 1984, 'Developing valuing and decision making skills in geography', in Fien, Gerber and Wilson, 1984, 29–43.

Mazey, H. and Lee, D., 1983, *Her Space, Her Place: a Geography of Women*, AAG, Washington.

McPherson, I., 1985, *Maps, Places and Faces*, Altered Image Publications, Surbiton.

Milburn, D., 1972, 'Children's vocabulary', in Graves, 1972, 107–20.

Mills, D. (ed.), 1981, *Geographical Work in Primary and Middle Schools*, The Geographical Association, Sheffield.

Milner, D., 1975, *Children and Race*, Penguin, Harmondsworth.

Morrill, R., 1985, 'Childhood geographies', *Journal of Geography*, 84, 3, 123–5.

Naish, M., 1982, 'Mental developments and the learning of geography', in Graves, 1982, 16–54.

Newson, E. and Newson, J., 1968, *Four Years Old in an Urban Community*, Allen & Unwin, London.

Newson, E. and Newson, J., 1978, *Seven Years Old in the Home Environment*, Penguin, Harmondsworth.

Oaks, S., 1974, 'A hydrology project in the primary school', *Geography*, 59, 65–7.

Orford, E., 1918, 'Geography: What facts shall we teach', *The Geographical Teacher*, 9, 212–15.

Owen, E. and Mason, G., 1980, 'The most visible countries and cities revisited', *The Journal of Geography*, 79, 5, 186–91.

Oxfam/Cockpit Arts Workshop, 1977, *The People Grid*, Oxfam, Oxford.

Palmer, M. and Wise, J., 1982, *The Good, the Bad and the Ugly*, Geographical Association, Sheffield.

Pattison, W., 1964, 'The four traditions of geography', *Journal of Geography*, 63, 211–16.

Piaget, J., 1955, *The Child's Construction of Reality*, Routledge & Kegan Paul, London.

Piaget, J. and Inhelder, B., 1956, *The Child's Conception of Space*, Routledge & Kegan Paul, London.

Piaget, J., Inhelder, B. and Szeminska, A., 1960, *The Child's Conception of Geometry*, Routledge & Kegan Paul, London.

Pocock, D. and Hudson, R., 1978, *Images of the Urban Environment*, Macmillan, London.

Prosser, P., 1982, *The World on Your Doorstep*, McGraw Hill, London.

Rampton, A., 1981, *West Indian Children in Our Schools*, HMSO, London.

Renwick, M. and Pick, B., 1979, *Going Places*, Nelson, Walton-on-Thames.

Sandford, H., 1986, 'Atlases and atlas mapwork', in Boardman, 1986, 139–44.

Schools Council, 1979, *Understanding Maps*, Schools Council, London.

Scoffham, S., 1980, *Using the School's Surroundings*, Ward Lock, London.

Seefeldt, C., 1977, *Social Studies for the Preschool-Primary Child*, Merrill, Columbus, Ohio.

Slater, F. and Weller, M., 1982, *Skills in Geography*, I, Cassell, London.

Spencer, D. and Lloyd, J., 1974, *A Child's Eye View of Small Heath, Birmingham*, Research Memorandum 34, Centre for Urban and Regional Studies, University of Birmingham.

Stephenson, B., 1984, 'Language in the geography classroom', in Fien, Gerber and Wilson, 1984, 13–28.

Storm, M., 1970, 'Schools and the community', *Bulletin of Environmental Education*, 1.

Storm, M., 1984, 'Teaching about minorities', in Fyson, 1984, 69.

Storm, M., 1986, 'The Peters mystery', *ILEA Geography Bulletin*, 24, 16–17.

Stradling, R., Noctor, M. and Baines, B., 1984, *Teaching Controversial Issues*, Arnold, London.

Tapsfield, A., 1984a, 'Primarily geography', in Watson, 1984.

Tapsfield, A., 1984b, *Micromapping I*, Nelcal, Nelson, London.

Walford, R., 1969, *Games in Geography*, Longman, London.

Walford, R. (ed.), 1973, *New Directions in Geography Teaching*, Longman, London.

Walford, R. (ed.), 1981a, *Signposts for Geography Teaching*, Longman, London.

Walford, R., 1981b, 'Games and simulations', in Mills, 1981.

Walford, R. (ed.), 1985, *Geographical Education for a Multicultural Society*, The Geographical Association, Sheffield.

Walford, R. and Taylor, S., 1972, *Simulation in the Classroom*, Penguin, Harmondsworth.

Watson, D. (ed.), 1984, *Exploring Geography with Microcomputers*, CET, London.

Williams, M. (ed.), 1981, *Geography: Language, Teaching and Learning*, Ward Lock, London.

Wilson, P., 1981, 'The map reasoning development of 8, 10 and 11 year old pupils as revealed in free recall sketch maps', in Wilson, Gerber and Fien, 1981, 143–99.

Wilson, P., Gerber, R. and Fien, J. (eds), 1981, *Research in*

Bibliography

Geographical Education, AGERA, Brisbane.
Wright, D., 1985, 'Evaluating Textbooks', in Boardman, 1985, 92–5.

Index

Index

Index